# NATURE
# OF
# MANAGEMENT

# CASE STUDIES

Edited by
Bill Braddick

First published 1985

© The Institute of Bankers, 1985

ISBN 0-85297-141-9

Cartoons by Ben Shailo

British Library Cataloguing in Publication Data

Nature of Management Case Studies

1.

2.

Cover: Chromocard 200gm²
Text paper: Dundee offset 90gm²
Typeset in 10 on 11pt Times and
printed and bound by Dramrite Printers Ltd, Southwark, London SE1, England.

# NATURE OF MANAGEMENT
## CASE STUDIES

## CONTENTS

# CONTENTS (Continued)

# FOREWORD

This book of case studies has been commissioned by The Institute of Bankers to help those who are studying for the Nature of Management paper in Stage 2 of the Institute's Examinations. It will also be useful to those who are studying for the Human Aspects of Management paper in the Financial Studies Diploma. It is hoped that further volumes will appear in due course.

Most of the cases have been written by Brian Stone of the Manchester Polytechnic and his two associates, Jane Barbour and Stephen Godby — to whom I owe the warmest thanks for their efforts, their skill and their patience. Without them this book would never have appeared. I should also like to thank Mike Henderson, Dave Cooper and Gerald Cohen for their very practical and useful contributions.

My thanks are also due to Rosemary Conway-Hyde for her typing, organisation and control of the cases as they appeared, and also to David Whelpton for his proof-reading.

No attempt has been made to classify these cases under headings. It is in the nature of management that problems do not fall neatly into categories. Nor do these cases.

A structure is suggested in the introduction to guide students in the ways they might tackle cases. Naturally, this structure is not always appropriate and it is offered as a means of approach rather than a rigid framework for analysis.

Bill Braddick
May 1985

# INTRODUCTION

The two courses of study concerned with management in The Institute of Bankers' curriculum are designed to help students to acquire some of the basic knowledge which is essential to a successful career in management. Knowledge alone is not enough. Managers not only have to know, they have to act. What they do varies widely, but their central concern is with making decisions which will allow their business to develop. The decisions they reach will often draw on a wide range of knowledge both technical and managerial. The skilful manager will be able to pull this knowledge together, identify the key elements of a problem, analyse what he must do, recognise alternative possibilities and then decide on the course of action which seems to be the most appropriate given all the factors involved.

It is to encourage the development of the application of this skill of logical analysis to a managerial situation that the case study is used in The Institute of Bankers examinations.

The case study helps to develop these skills by providing a descriptive, realistic managerial situation in some of its complexity. To solve the case study students must develop their problem-solving skills. They must learn to weigh evidence, to analyse a situation in detail and to be able to choose a decision from a number of possible alternatives which they can argue and defend. Ideally the use of case studies should develop the ability to see the problem as a whole and encourage the ability to conceptualise and synthesise.

There are other important advantages to be gained. Students learn to ask searching questions. They learn to distinguish fact from fiction and symptoms from causes. If they are to produce useful solutions they must also be able to weigh the quality and the relative importance of different pieces of data, and they must handle a range of variables simultaneously and come to some conclusion about their relative importance.

If the case study is used in the classroom as a basis for discussion and debate to encourage skills and abilities, other advantages accrue. Discussion of cases with one's peers encourages the student to recognise that there are many alternative interpretations of the same basic facts and that there is more than one right answer. If they listen to the views of other people it becomes evident that there is more than one way of looking at a situation. This can do much to encourage a more flexible attitude, greater tolerance of others, and a willingness to come to decisions in conditions of ambiguity. The use of case studies has many benefits, some clear, some hidden, both for the individual working alone, and also as a basis for group study. Full value depends, though, on the skills of the teacher and on the willingness of the student to develop the skills of systematic analysis.

## THE TEACHER

For the teacher, the overriding questions in the preparation of a lesson are the simple ones. What do I want to achieve? What is the best method to use to make sure I gain my objective? Sometimes the case is the best means to achieve the objective, but on other occasions there will be more appropriate methods. Even if the case is the most appropriate, it should be chosen with care to suit the experience and stage of development of the student and it is probably wise not to introduce it into the course at too early a stage. Students should have at least a basic framework for thinking about the subject of management before plunging into its complexities. Comparatively simple cases can be used to introduce the method and more complicated ones can be used later in the course. All the cases in this book have been written with the specific needs of banking students in mind. Nevertheless teachers must decide whether, within the pressures of a very full syllabus, the time which a full discussion takes in class can be justified.

Alternatively they might consider that cases are best used as a basis for written work at home. This will encourage the development of individual skills, but will deprive the students of the opportunity of pitting their ideas against those of others.

The case study requires particular teaching skills to get out all the lessons which should be learnt. First, the case must be closely studied and read. The teacher must do his own analysis and come to his own tentative conclusions, but keep an open enough mind to encourage the debate of alternative views. The successful case teacher needs to give enough leadership to encourage stimulating discussion and debate while avoiding the suggestion of an inevitable and right conclusion. Leadership must be combined with an ability to encourage discussion, the development of a number of alternative courses of action and guidance towards a realistic solution. Finally, concepts and generalisations which can be deduced from the case need to be drawn out and discussed.

### KEY QUESTIONS FOR THE TEACHER

1. What is the objective of this session. What do I want students to learn?
2. Is the use of the case study the best means of achieving the learning objective or is there a more appropriate method?
3. Am I familiar enough with this case to be able to lead a comprehensive discussion?
4. How will I get the best out of this case?
   — individual preparation and written answer
   — individual preparation and full class discussion
   — syndicate work and plenary discussion
   — role playing?

5.   Have I a clear structure which students can learn to use in their own case analysis?

6.   What lessons of general applicability can I draw from this specific example?

## THE STUDENT

The aim of the case study is to help the student to acquire a major managerial skill — the ability to understand the issues involved in a managerial situation, and to analyse it systematically to produce a workable solution from a range of alternatives. A case study consists of a description of a problem which a manager has to solve. As such, any of the usual methods of problem analysis and solution can be applied. One approach is offered below. Before tackling a case however, students should read the case two or three times to ensure that they are familiar with the facts and that they have fully grasped the implications of the case.

## CASE ANALYSIS

A useful structure for analysis is to ask the following questions

1.   What is the evidence that a problem exists?

2.   What is the precise nature of the problem?

3.   What are the causes of the problem and what are the symptoms?

4.   What are the key issues and why are they important?

5.   Who must deal with the problem?

6.   What should their aim be?

7.   What possible courses of action are there?

8.   What are the advantages and disadvantages of each?

9.   What is the best solution in the light of all the evidence?

10.  What are the likely effects. Can anything be done to anticipate any negative outcomes?

11.  When should there be follow-up action and who should take it?

If you use these case studies in class discussion keep an open mind when you take part in the discussion. Try to see how equally valid deductions can be made from the same facts. Listen for a logical analysis, careful argument and practical solutions. Learn from this to improve your own skill, not only in doing case studies, but as a step to becoming a good manager.

# CASE STUDY 1

John Cooper, a twenty year old who joined the bank straight from school with two 'A' levels, has been working as the standing order clerk at your branch for the past three months after a successful spell of six months as a counter clerk, at which he had a justifiable reputation for speed and accuracy. His predecessor in the standing orders job was Anne Macdonald, a twenty-five year old, who left the branch to take maternity leave just as John was beginning to get to know the work. She had given John his basic training having herself been trained about a year earlier. When John took over the post on his own he had reported to his immediate supervisor, the chief clerk of the branch, that much of the work from the previous month had not been done. The chief clerk was rather surprised that the apparently efficient Mrs. Macdonald had not been more up-to-date with her work. He encouraged John to work a couple of hours overtime each night for the first week-and-a-half to clear the backlog. John was not very happy to work overtime and after the period ended, he always stopped work at about the same time as the counter staff, one of whom regularly gave him a lift to and from work.

Over the last two weeks the branch manager has received letters from four different customers complaining of errors made by the bank in their standing orders. In each case the branch had been sent instructions by letter nearly two months ago and the standing orders should have been set up to make the first payments during the past few weeks. In one case the bank continued to pay a standing order which should have been cancelled and the customer involved, Major Wellings, threatened to close his account if the bank made a similar mistake again. Major Wellings had been an account holder for many years and was also a director of a small manufacturing company in the area. The company account, held at another branch of the bank, was considered very valuable because of the high credit balances which the business had built up over its long history.

In response to these complaints the manager instructed the chief clerk, Mr. Farrell, to find out what was going on and sort out the problem as quickly as possible in case there were other mistakes which had not yet come to light. As chief clerk Mr. Farrell was in charge of the work of about a third of the twenty-five staff at the branch, all those not directly answerable to either the chief cashier or the supervisor of the machine room. He had been moved to the branch three years earlier and was hoping for a further promotion before very long since he had a good reputation for coming up with effective new marketing ideas. Branch profitability improved and the increasing targets set by head office had regularly been met during his time at the branch.

Following the manager's instructions, Mr. Farrell had decided to begin by considering the procedures involved before tackling John about the matter. He suspected that the computer terminal operators might be entering information incorrectly because they were unable to read the writing on the computer data forms which John had to fill in. John's writing was often untidy but the other clerks were used to this and were not aware of any particular problem, and in any case the data input sheets were checked against the computer printout on the following day so a third person had an opportunity to pick up any errors and arrange for them to be corrected.

Mr. Farrell also considered the possibility that mail distribution within the branch might be at fault. But he ruled this out as the cause of the problem since he regularly took the letters round to the staff himself as a way of keeping in touch with his section. He rarely had time to check on the work of his junior staff during the branch's open hours, particularly since he had been so busy recently, putting right mistakes made by one of the clerks dealing with new accounts. He did however find out that the letters to which John had apparently failed to respond were not in the respective customers' files. There was no evidence that any reply or acknowledgement had been sent or that any other action had been taken although there seemed no doubt that the letters did reach the standing order desk.

If you were the branch manager what would you do about this problem?

# CASE STUDY 1 – MODEL ANSWER

**Aim**    To improve customer services by ensuring that all standing order instructions are carried out accurately within the time period specified.

**Problem**    A series of errors by the standing orders clerk.

**Causes**    1.  The underlying problem is one of control.

(a)  Control systems do not appear to be implemented

(b)  Supervisory responsibility is confused

(c)  Performance standards are lax

(d)  No training has been given.

2.  Data to support this view includes:

(a)  The chief clerk's surprise at the backlog.

(b)  His lack of time for checking on the work of junior staff.

(c)  His involvement in correcting errors.

(d)  His preoccupation with other issues, e.g. marketing

(e)  His follow-up of the false lead about errors to do with data checking.

(f)  Confusion over supervisory responsibility.

**Analysis**    John has received inadequate supervision from the chief clerk to whom he directly reports. The chief clerk seems not to be aware of the extent of the problem. He does not monitor performance. He is pre-occupied with 'marketing' issues at the expense of his supervisory duties.

**Solution**    1.  An examination of the work of the chief clerk to check whether he:

(a)  is genuinely overworked and therefore has not the time to supervise correctly.

(b)  uses his time inefficiently.

(c)  has never been trained and coached to work effectively as a supervisor.

(d)  is not a suitable choice as a supervisor.

The branch manager will have to decide on a course of action when he is clear as to which of these factors explains the behaviouir.

2.  John must be taught to do the job correctly

(a)  He must be set clear performance standards

(b)  He must be given short term goals to achieve these standards

(c)  Effective measures must be established to monitor his work

(d)  He must be given frequent feedback, coaching and training to enable him to achieve his performance standards.

# CASE STUDY 2

You work for a major UK clearing bank with an extensive branch network. A pilot scheme is in progress in one city within your region. The scheme involves the removal of branch managers from smaller suburban branches to work under a 'chief manager' at a number of major branches.

The move has left senior clerks, used to working directly under a manager, in day-to-day control of the smaller branches. Some clerical functions have been centralised and managers only visit the branches they remain responsible for when customers cannot call at chief office.

The timetable of introduction has been rapid:

## 6 months ago

The regional manager was told that the Chief Executive wanted to run the pilot scheme in a city in his region.

Operations and methods staff were instructed to select the most geographically suitable city and prepare a scheme showing 'chief branches' and their proposed subordinate branches.

The time-scale was such that detailed examination of the individual branch resources was not feasible

## 4 months ago

The regional manager was given the Operations and Methods Report and instructed by the executive to bring a scheme into effect as soon as possible.

## 3 months ago

The branch managers involved were briefed on the plan and their changed responsibilities. A maildrop was despatched advising customers where to contact their manager. It assured them that their day-to-day banking requirements would be catered for at their local branches.

## 2½ months ago

Branch staff informed by circular.

## 1 month ago

New system started.

Managers involved in the scheme have expressed great surprise that the transition has been achieved so quickly and successfully. They have found that under the new system they have easier access to backup services for appraisal of propositions, marketing, research and legal advice. They feel freed from mundane aspects of daily accounting routines and staff control.

## CASE STUDY 2

Customers have given the scheme a mixed reception. Major corporate customers have accepted the transition very readily but a few personal customers have expressed dissatisfaction at having to travel to a 'chief branch' or having to wait for a reply to a relatively simple proposition. The new arrangements have on the whole not produced any major customer opposition.

You are in a senior clerical grade and at a recent regional staff function you met four colleagues at a similar grade who are involved with the pilot scheme. All four have been left in day to day control of their branches, which are of a similar size, and their managers now operate from 'chief branches'. You are interested in their different reactions:

### John Archbold

John is aged 44 and was only transferred to his current branch ten months ago. He has previously worked for six years in a specialist head office department.

John is very unhappy with the situation. He complains that he does not feel able to keep on top of the job without guidance. Productivity levels and quality of service have fallen off seriously in the last month. He is seriously considering requesting a move to other duties.

### David Baker

David is aged 30, having entered the bank from university. He has been in his present job for three years. He is very pleased with the pilot scheme as before its inception he had felt frustrated working under a manager. He now finds the increased freedom and responsibility a great motivator. He feels he has a good opportunity to use initiative and to show his potential for promotion. He does, however, feel confused at times about the extent of his authority and responsibility.

### Arthur Crabtree

Arthur has worked in the same branch all his working career and at 54 was quite happy to see out his remaining service as the invaluable right-hand man to the manager. He now feels thrust into the role of a manager and does not know what is expected of him. The branch runs smoothly but he will not make decisions on anything but the most minor of propositions.

### Joan Dodsworth

Is aged 39 and has been at the branch for two years. Previously she worked in rural branches. With the move of her manager to chief office she is left in charge of a branch staff of six, of which five are male. The branch is situated in a heavily industrialised area. Joan admits to being unhappy with the response she gets from both staff and customers; she misses the support of a manager.

# CASE STUDY 2

All four of your colleagues complain that they were not given any warning of the proposed change and no preparation. They are very critical of the introduction. Interestingly they report that their staff have accepted the change with little comment and no complaint. When asked, three out of four of your friends stated they would prefer to work under the old system rather than under the new scheme.

Whilst managers, junior staff and customers generally seem happy with the new approach, colleagues at your level are dissatisfied.

Analyse the problem and suggest ways it could have been avoided, put forward a plan to remove the dissatisfaction.

NB: It is not intended that the four individuals should be looked at separately in terms of motivation and leadership, etc.

PRETENDING TO BE MANAGER

# CASE STUDY 2 – MODEL ANSWER

**The Problem**    Three out of four senior clerks from differing backgrounds are dissatisfied with the way in which their jobs have been changed as a result of the new scheme. Doubts and misgivings exist about the extent of their responsibility and authority under the new system.

The underlying cause of the dissatisfaction should become evident on examining the case study:

Clerks previously working directly under a manager now are the senior person in the branch most of the time. The nature of the senior clerk's job has therefore changed. However, little attention has been given to the nature of the job and in particular:

(a)    No *selection procedures* were used. The present incumbents have merely 'inherited' a changed task. Of the four persons described three are obviously not well suited to their new role.

(b)    No *training* or guidance has been given to prepare the senior clerk for the new role.

(c)    There seems to have been little *research* before the introduction of the scheme particularly *with reference to staff resources*. Poor *communication* is indicated by the apparent ignorance by managers of senior clerks' dissatisfaction. Poor communication is also underlined by the fact that customers were advised of the changes before most staff.

**Avoidance**    The problem could have been avoided by:

1.    A longer timescale for implementation allowing more time for research and communication. In particular, the manpower implications of the pilot scheme should have been carefully examined.

2.    *Selection.* Redefinition was required of the senior clerks' *job description*; and a new *personnel specification* was needed. This is likely to have laid greater stress on qualities such as:

(i)    Initiative

(ii)   Leadership

(iii)  Decision making/problem solving

(iv)   Delegation

The present incumbents and/or alternative job holders should have been *assessed* against the required standard.

3.  Clear goals and performance standards should be set and regular feedback should be given.

4.  *Training.* Comparisons of achievement against standard for the new role would highlight training needs.

The new role may require new or improved skills in the following areas:

(i)    Staff management

(ii)   Customer contact

(iii)  Lending/technical skills

(iv)   Report skills

5.  Training might typically involve role-play exercises and case study work as well as coaching and counselling.

**Removing the dissatisfaction**

Management should remove the dissatisfaction before it manifests itself in poor quality work, absenteeism, transfer requests and possible resignations.

Their *alternative courses of action* are to:

(a)  Abandon the scheme and revert to previous sytems.

(b)  Draft standards required in the new job, setting-up training/assessment courses to compare existing and potential job holders with the specification.

Alternative (a) would no doubt satisfy most of the senior clerks but, as the scheme seems otherwise a success, it would appear to be too great a sacrifice.

(b) would appear more realistic: problems here would be those of motivating the incumbents to undertake the courses or new assignments. Providing cover in the office whilst the courses are run would be a logistical problem.

**Conclusion**   The case study highlights the importance of manpower planning in any organisation. It underlines the fact that changes in organisational structure cannot be considered in isolation as they will have a bearing on staffing. Selection, assessment and training must be considered when adjusting structure. Taking the time to plan staff resources and how they will be affected by changes is time well spent.

# CASE STUDY 3

David Smith is the supervisor of a busy new clerical section set up in your bank six months ago. He has six clerks under his supervision: one senior clerk and five juniors. Each junior has different regular tasks to perform, all of which interlink and each of which is understood by the senior man of the six. He covers for them occasionally and is competent in every job, although he lacks sufficient experience and knowledge to tackle more complex technical matters.

Smith, on the other hand, can not only do all the clerical jobs in the section but he also takes sole responsibility for more complicated work. He supervises the output of all the staff very closely; so closely, that they joke about it to the senior clerk and complain to each other about Smith's constant attention. This leads to resentment on the part of the senior clerk, who feels that his authority is constantly undermined.

As a rule, all the clerks complete their day's work between 1630 and 1700 hrs. David Smith, on the other hand, rarely finishes before 1830, and has little time for lunch, because he is so busy checking the section's work as well as completing his own.

Recently the section had a disastrous week, when Smith was off work owing to illness. The senior clerk had never had a chance to deputise for Smith and therefore was simply unable to handle his more difficult work; and because of Smith's normal methods of operation, the senior clerk had no experience of effectively supervising the running of the section. On several occasions the manager had to step in to solve time-consuming problems, some of which in fact could not be solved at all without the presence of Smith.

On his return to work, Smith was told by the manager in no uncertain terms of the damage caused by the inefficiency and disorganisation of his section. His poor performance as a supervisor meant that his section ran very badly without him. His reaction was one of shock and dismay. He felt he had worked hard, had put in extra hours, was extremely conscientious about the quality of the section's work, and concerned to save his staff excessive effort. In his distress, however, he indicated a willingness to try to see to it that the situation would never arise again.

What should Smith's manager do to help him? What steps should Smith himself take?

# CASE STUDY 3 – MODEL ANSWER

**Problem**

1. Insufficient delegation of tasks by Smith.

2. No planning for contingencies such as absence of key personnel.

3. Skills poorly distributed; little if any emphasis on training.

4. Poor use of time: staff finished early, supervisor works excessive overtime.

5. Supervisory role and responsibilities of senior clerk unclear.

6. Supervision too close, leading to resentment of all section staff.

7. Supervisor has failed as 'linking pin" between section and management. He discovered problem-situation only in emergency.

**Suggested Solution:**

*Manager*

— check Smith's training in supervisory work; check availability of such training in the bank; arrange for a place for Smith.

— Discuss supervisory responsibility with Smith: the nature of management and responsibilities other than technical.

— Suggest Smith takes time to define his own responsibilities, and draw up short and longer-term plans for the manning of his section, and contingency plans for holidays and staffing emergencies, etc.

— Monitor; set performance goals with Smith for himself and his section and discuss progress and encourage further development.

*Smith*

— explain immediately to his team the nature of the problem and the need to improve performance.

— Review problems and causes. Accept responsibility; and request cooperation.

— Inform group that changes are proposed which will result in more interesting work and opportunities for development.

— Plan changes along the following lines:

(a) Introduce job rotation to widen knowledge and skills of the whole group to provide stimulus and interest.

(b) Use training department courses and reinforce skills by on-job training. Set training schedule and targets.

(c) Discuss and agree role of senior clerk.

(d) Set performance standards; monitor regularly, and ensure that the five others work to the senior clerk and take problems to him.

(e) Keep management informed on a regular basis of progress in the work of the section. Enlist their help if difficulties arise or are foreseen.

# CASE STUDY 4

The newly appointed Equipment Officer in the Royal Bank of Manchester is faced with a problem in the Personnel Department office concerning a new word-processor.

Yesterday, in all good faith, he went to the personnel office, and no sooner had he arrived when the Personnel Manager called him in, and in no uncertain terms told him what the prevailing opinion was of the Equipment Office in particular and of word-processors in general. It eventually became clear that the machine had been delivered and set up without warning and with only a very brief description of its functions. Furthermore, the personnel secretary was expected to learn how to use it straight away.

The equipment officer spoke to the secretary. She was very upset and was quite definite about the word-processor. She would not go anywhere near it. She said it was too complicated; she didn't see why a typewriter was not good enough. She understood she might get headaches from it. She thought it might take her job away from her; and she had reported the whole thing to the union, who were actively considering the case.

Things would not have been so bad, if she had known something about the imminent arrival of the machine. She had been trained and had gained her experience on a conventional typewriter, and she had heard of word-processors without forming any views on them. The first one she had seen was this one which had come a few days ago, so unexpected and so unwelcome.

The equipment officer then went to delivery department, who supplied and delivered the machine, and told the manager about the incident. In the latter's opinion a lot of fuss was being made about nothing. The girl should be told that the word-processor was just an elaborate typewriter and she should pull herself together and get on with it. She should think herself lucky, he said, that the deliveryman was no ordinary van-driver but also set it up and showed her how to use it.

Finally, it was made clear to the equipment officer by his own manager that the machine in the personnel office was there to be used whether they liked it or not. As a matter of bank policy many more machines would have to be introduced over the next six months; and it would be the equipment department's job to make sure that they became operational as soon as possible. When the equipment officer asked about whose responsibility it was to install the machines, to check that they worked and to train the operators, it transpired that nobody had really defined and allocated these tasks.

What should the equipment officer do (a) about the current situation in the personnel office, (b) to make the introduction of other word-processors more effective?

# CASE STUDY 4 — MODEL ANSWER

**Problem** — lack of coordination of various functions in the supply and installation of word-processors.

— lack of information/briefing from the Headquarters to managers, from managers to staff, on new technology.

— No arrangements for off-job or on-job training.

— Unhelpful attitude by manager of delivery department.

**Solutions** (a) Current situation

*Senior Management*

Obtain clear definition of various responsibilities, e.g. managers to brief; equipment office to obtain/coordinate all activities; delivery to install and check.

*Personnel manager*

Explain how the secretary is to be trained and encouraged to use the word-processor.

*Secretary*

Arrange IMMEDIATE introduction to word-processor by an expert OR by a secretary currently using one;

Show her the career advantages of being a word-processor operator within and outside banking career;

Show her the benefits in her current work, and to personnel office, of word-processor capabilities.

Arrange full-scale formal course, in agreement with management (in-house if bank so provides, or external if necessary).

Speak to her and union about withdrawal of complaint for the time being. Clarify management and union agreement and procedures for introduction of new technology.

(b)   Future

*Training Department*

Discuss formal training for secretaries of departments due to receive word-processors. Set in hand as soon as possible.

*Recipients*

All will receive a visit prior to the introduction by an experienced operator to introduce the idea of the machine, show benefits, and arrange training. Obtain or write short, simple introduction to word-processing to leave with those visited.

*Delivery manager*

Obtain delivery schedule; agree changes if necessary to give time for introductions. Arrange that equipment manager speaks with him about attitude so as not to cause problems in sensitive areas.

*Equipment office*

Check that all colleagues in own office aware of new procedure.

# CASE STUDY 5

You are a senior clerk in a large branch bank in a provincial town. Your manager has decided that customer service should be improved and has formed a committee of junior staff to discuss and present suggestions to the management in a month's time.

You are a member of this committee, but not the chairperson, who is a young lady a grade junior to you. She was most reluctant to take the responsibility, because, as she said, she had never even been to many meetings, never mind chaired any. However, she was offered no choice in the matter: the manager simply appointed her.

In fact she could be quite a good choice. She is an experienced cashier known to the public as efficient and pleasant, and she has often expressed strong views about the importance of good service. She is by no means shy; she often takes the lead and sometimes dominates a conversation. She thinks of herself as intelligent and logical, and sometimes puts people down quite firmly if she finds flaws in their arguments.

You were unable to go to the first meeting of the committee, but from what you hear it was not at all successful. In conversation with those present you have gained the impression that progress was slow and difficult. The chairperson tended to be aggressive. Very few ideas emerged, and it was not too clear to those present what they were there to achieve.

You have also talked to the chairperson. She thinks that nobody was forthcoming or enthusiastic enough. They all kept going off the subject and asking silly questions. Such ideas as there were turned out to be trivial or irrelevant in her opinion, apart from the ones she had to suggest herself. She confided that she was worried about the next meeting, about the likely success of the committee in general, and indeed about her overall relationships with the staff who were committee members.

The next meeting is to take place in a week's time. What can you do to ensure that the committee performs more effectively when it next meets.

# CASE STUDY 5 — MODEL ANSWER

**The Problem**   The failure of the first committee meeting.

Probable causes of failure of first meeting:

1. Objectives unclear even to chairperson.
2. Meetings not properly planned in advance.
3. Chairperson does not understand her own role.
4. The chairperson not thought carefully enough about the committee members.

**Solutions**

1. Talk with the chairperson to:

    (a) clarify the objectives of the committee, spell out its terms of reference and identify the authority of the chairperson;

    (b) help her to plan the next meeting by having an agenda circulated in advance;

    (c) help her to think through each agenda item so that she can encourage useful discussions;

    (d) explain and clarify the role of a chairperson as someone who leads and controls a meeting to drawout and develop the ideas of its members. Correct the impression that the chairperson is there to impose his/her ideas on the meeting;

    (e) Get her to have the decisions of the meeting recorded and circulated;

    (f) Persuade her to think of the knowledge and experience of committee members before the meeting so that she can draw upon it during the meeting.

2. Brief all committee members on the:

    (a) objective of the committee;

    (b) the role of the chairperson;

    (c) the ways in which they can make an effective contribution;

    (d) get a secretary appointed to record the proceedings and circulate a record of them

3. Attend the next meeting and afterwards give feedback to the chairperson and the committee members about the effectiveness of the meeting and what they can do to improve the next one.

# CASE STUDY 6

The machine room in your branch is upstairs, some way from the office. There has been little change of staff for about eighteen months, and the branch has been so busy that little attention has been paid to a programme of job rotation suggested by the manager about two years ago. He has now been transferred, and a new, inexperienced manager has arrived and made some changes.

Until nine months ago the girls in the machine room had worked together for at least a year. While they were somewhat bored with the tasks — and said so to all who would listen, including the new manager — they nevertheless got on well together. They were known as the "A-team", were effective at the job and enjoyed working together.

The new manager had spent some time touring the branch, talking to the staff and observing their ways of work before preparing a reorganisation programme which he promised would make the branch more effective. When he finished his tour nine months ago he announced his new plans.

Before doing so he was overhead talking to a visit from head office. "It's amazing", he said, "How the girls in the machine room spend all day chatting. They should be getting on with the work." He added: "I'll soon cut that out. They'll soon find out that terminal-work isn't the only boring job in the branch."

The new plans were announced. They included a rigorous programme of job rotation. No member of staff was allowed to spend more than three months on one particular job. No team was to be allowed to be together for more than three months either. The terminals were moved and so arranged, by the clever use of screening, that the terminal operators only talk to each other with difficulty.

To the new manager's surprise, the changes have not resulted in improved productivity. On the contrary, an increase in the overtime has occurred with no improvement in business. There has been an increase in absenteeism and minor sicknesses, an increase in error rate and a noticeable reduction in morale.

The manager can't understand it. "I only put these plans in to improve efficiency, to revitalise these people, and give them something interesting to do — and to cut out idle chatter and so on. I can't think why they don't react better to my efforts."

Can you? What would you do now?

# CASE STUDY 6 — MODEL ANSWER

**Problem**     (a)     Symptoms

The 'improved' working practices have resulted in reduced output:

— more time spent doing the same amount of work (overtime)

— increased absenteeism — the withdrawal of labour for trivial reasons

— low morale, probably noticeable in "atmosphere": reduction in informal communication

— more mistakes.

(b)     Causes

The experiments in the Hawthorne Works of the Western Electrical Company in the 1920s, in which girls worked together in an experimental group as opposed to working individually, indicated that it was the group-work that had a greater effect on productivity than other changes instituted. The experimenters concluded that:

— Work is a group activity and people need to enter into relationships with each other. The work-group is an important satisfier of our need for belonging, warmth and security.

— Being selected as, or recognised as, special has a positive effect on productivity. To be seen as an effective team contributes further to that effectiveness.

— People like to have to be consulted about, and to help make decisions about, their work and their time.

— Complaints are, more frequently than many managers suspect, symptoms of deeper problems.

The manager of this branch may also be unaware that people need to satisfy their Social, or Belonging, needs by being able to identify themselves as members of a clearly delineated group; and they need to satisfy Ego or Self-esteem needs by becoming good at, and being recognised as good at, tasks which are necessary for the success of their group. This is hard to do when you are being frequently moved. It is also hard in such conditions to feel any sense of achievement, to feel that one is learning, growing and developing.

**Solutions**
Job-rotation is not necessarily either effective or ineffective. It, like many other management tools, might solve some types of problem.

Cliques are harmful only if their existence causes resentment or results in undeserved privileges and produces lower morale, either inside or outside the group.

There is no evidence in this case that 'A-team' membership was causing any reduction in effectiveness, nor that their propensity to chat was impeding the work flow.

Furthermore, while boredom either in the machine room or elsewhere in the branch can be a problem, job-rotation is not necessarily the answer. Sometimes the job can be enriched by giving the job holders special projects which create the opportunities for them to learn.

Whatever changes are proposed, staff should be consulted to gain their cooperation, their commitment and their help in the planning and implementation of new ideas.

Finally, no scheme in which rotation in jobs is called for should permit changes before the operative has had time to become proficient. This is because the development of new skills is very important to people.

Change for its own sake is not very productive. It should be introduced with clear business objectives in mind, preferably those which engage the commitment of staff.

# CASE STUDY 7

June Harrison is a junior clerk at the Hightown branch of a major bank where she has worked for the last eight years. She is sound and dependable and can be relied on to perform her tasks with diligence and enthusiasm. She is happy in her work, contented at the branch, and has no ambition for advancement according to her annual appraisals.

In recent weeks there has been a deterioration in both the quality and the quantity of her work, so that it is now barely adequate. She has withdrawn from her relationship with her fellow clerks. Her immediately senior clerk, Mary Winton, has noticed both the decline in work-standards and her change in spirits.

Until recently both girls had worked together on the same grade and had been friends within the office, though they did not mix socially. Last month, however, Mary was promoted one grade, and while June seemed pleased at the time, Mary thought that June might resent the promotion, and this might be the cause of the change in her behaviour.

Mary felt very diffident about approaching June directly about this, so she approached her assistant manager, Derek Booth, to tell him about June and to ask him to have a word to find out what was wrong and what could be done about it. Booth made it quite clear that he did not really want to become involved in some "silly women's squabble", but he added that if June's work was not up to scratch he would soon sort her out. Somewhat taken aback by this aggressive response, Mary left without adding anything to the conversation.

Booth's well advertised attitude was that staff were well-paid and had good conditions. They should therefore be expected to perform well at all times. He also believed that they were well trained and should not need constant mollycoddling. For this reason he did not know the staff well and rarely checked their progress except to correct their mistakes, which he did firmly. He called June into the office, and told her that she was not pulling her weight, and if she didn't pull her socks up she might be on report to head office. June's immediate response was to burst into tears; and Booth called Mary in to "calm the silly emotional woman down".

At 0855 the following morning Booth received a telephone call from June's husband to say that June would not be coming to work because she was too ill and upset. He went on to say that he considered Booth insensitive and callous, especially in view of her father's serious illness. Before Booth could respond, Mr. Harrison had slammed the telephone down.

Booth's immediate response was to call Mary in. "Why on earth didn't you tell me June's father was ill? You've made me look a complete fool" he said. Mary was overwhelmed by the news, which of course probably explained June's recent behaviour.

## CASE STUDY 7

Mary now felt guilty in going to Booth in the first place; she felt bad about not being sympathetic towards June and she didn't know how to approach June to sort things out. The upset must have shown in her face, because the last thing she heard as Booth left the room was, "Not another one! I am I fed up with weeping women ..."

What do you consider to be the weaknesses in the way in which this whole matter was handled? How could it have been handled more effectively?

# CASE STUDY 7 — MODEL ANSWER

**Problem**  June's work has deteriorated to a standard which is only just acceptable. If this is allowed to go on the work of the section will suffer. Neither Booth nor Mary for different reasons have discovered why June is working badly. The causes for their failure seems to derive from:

(a)  Booth's managerial style. Because he is basically authoritarian, he had not attempted to explain Mary's promotion to June, nor had he made any attempt to find out why her work had deteriorated.

(b)  His approach to problem-solving reflects this style. He acted intuitively on Mary's unconfirmed report. He made no attempt to find out the facts, analyse the situation and produce a realistic plan of action.

(c)  He has a crude understanding of what motivates people at work and this colours the way he treats them. Nor does he seem to understand the need to get people to work as a team.

(d)  He has not given Mary any help, coaching or counselling in her new role and as a result she does the job inadequately.

**Solutions**  A more effective treatment of the situation might have included the following actions:

1.  Learning of the problem, Booth should have agreed that Mary was correct to have brought a possible problem to his attention and he should have taken time to discuss the matter and get all the details. He should have investigated the situation fully before talking to June.

2.  Before seeing June he should have:

— Read recent appraisals to discover her usual standard of performance.

— Checked personally on any falling-off of performance, by observation.

— Discussed the possible problem with the branch manager or previous assistant manager, if relevant.

3.   When he interviewed June he should have:

—    Adopted a sympathetic approach, contrasting her recent performance with her usual high standards.

—    Explored possible causes for the decline in performance, including the new relationship with Mary.

—    Emphasised the need for continuing high standards, but told her that time would be made available, and cover for her work, if her father needed attention by her during his illness.

4.   Follow-up:

—    Tell the manager and Mary of the outcome of the meeting.

—    Enlist Mary's support for June if she has to leave the office to attend to her father.

—    Check and monitor performance and take any necessary corrective action.

5.   The branch manager should take a greater interest in Booth's progress as an assistant manager and arrange for him to attend a management training course.

# CASE STUDY 8

James Petheridge has been the manager of Harrytown branch of your bank for ten years. He has been a manager for just over twenty years in all. He is a member of the 'Old School' of managers, a fact he will proudly claim for himself before he is accused of it.

In Harrytown, the old-fashioned way he runs his branch suits the customers very well, since most of them are wealthy and/or retired, and they like their bank manager to be in the mould so often portrayed in television situation comedies. His staff don't like his style.

He doesn't like some of the new ideas coming from head office. He will have nothing to do with competitions. When prizes were awarded recently for the most attractive office, Mr. Petheridge would not even enter. Business development is a foreign phrase as far as he is concerned: he would not ask his customers to use bank services unless they suggested it first. As a branch, Harrytown is low in all the area league-tables and practically static in growth.

While Mr. Petheridge attends Rotary evenings, he does not bother with any other local activities and he does not encourage his staff to do so: "If it is not worthy of the attention of the Bank Manager", he says (and you can hear the capital letters), "it isn't worthy of the bank."

He is firmly of the belief that the proper business of the banker is banking. While he is an absolute tyrant when it comes to the Institute's examinations and leans heavily on his staff to take and pass them, he cannot for the life of him understand why their efforts should be wasted on a paper like the Nature of Management when they could be studying something useful like an extra paper on securities or lending.

As for management training, he believes that the bank's programme is the last straw. In Harrytown branch there are at least two people at senior clerical level who could be nominated for management development, but when they asked about it, Mr. Petheridge called them in and made it quite clear what he thought about the whole concept.

He said he thought it was some airy-fairy American concept which had nothing to do with banking; that all you really needed was technical excellence because that's all the public needed; that people didn't — or shouldn't have — come into banks to compete and to be hard-nosed salesmen; that there was nothing you could learn on a management training course you couldn't learn in the 'University of Life'; and that he had made it to the managerial ranks on the basis of knowledge, experience and patience and he thought everyone else should do the same.

How can the two candidates for management development modify Mr. Petheridge's views about the need for management training and development.

CAPTAIN MAINWARING ... I MEAN MR PETHERIDGE

MANAGE

# CASE STUDY 8 — MODEL ANSWER

Mr. Petheridge's views are extremely old-fashioned. More and more managers, even of the old school, now acknowledge the developments in banking since the early 'seventies and have taken steps to develop themselves as well as their staff to meet modern commercial and managerial challenges.

In this case Mr. Petheridge needs to be approached tactfully and rationally, and as a first step the management development hopefuls may like first to review the situation:

**The Problem**    Mr. Petheridge has not seen the value of modern developments in motivation, business development and in particular in management training. In order to clarify these, he will have to be convinced of their value to him as a manager and to the two candidates in question as members of his own branch staff.

Careful consideration of the current position will reveal a lack of competitive standing of the branch, a gap between the attitudes of the staff and those of Mr. Petheridge leading possibly to less communication than would be desirable, a static business development position, and frustration among those who would like advancement in their careers. Morale is low and the staff are developing an unhealthy apathy towards the bank and its standing in the community.

**The Solution**    (a)    Simple dismissal of a branch manager's views will not correct them : a case must be carefully prepared. Convincing arguments should be worked out to show how management training for the staff would benefit the branch. Some of the following steps might be taken:

— Obtain details of the bank's management development programme and in particular the statement of its objectives.

— Speak to people who have been on the programme to clarify the aims and content of sessions.

— Clarify the stated benefits in terms of improved performance.

— If possible, speak confidentially to the bank's personnel or training staff about the programme and the procedure for nomination and selection.

— Prepare an argument for management development in terms of the direct and indirect benefits to the branch and the bank rather than to one's own personal career.

(b)    The case for management development

Some of the following elements may be used to support the case for management development :

*(i)    Organisational development*

An organisation must be able to cope with its environment. Until the late 1960s this could have been described as safe, stable, unchanging and predictable. Banks needed structures and staff to match the environment. They produced services which needed little in the way of energy or imagination.

More recently, the business climate has changed and become more volatile, competitive, fluctating and turbulent. This environment demands a more ''organic'' structure and approach, to be able to solve new and varying financial and business problems.

Staff cannot suddenly alter their skills, their personalities, their outlook: they must be recruited and then trained for the forecast needs to deal with their markets. In fact there is still room for mechanistic styles and skills — Mr. Petheridge's traditional customers, for instance, like the solid stability of his old-fashioned approach. There is, however, also the need for staff who can face new challenges.

*(ii)    Future staffing needs*

The aim of management development is to provide staff trained to meet future management requirements. Working with less-than-perfect predictions, staff are taken early in their careers and attempts are made to give them the knowledge and skill to cater for different future demands. Perhaps the best training for Mr. Petheridge's job was the one he had: but it may not be the best for those who will run the bank which pays his pension!

*(iii)    Currently useful non-technical skills*

Management training can develop skills which could be useful to the branch in the present as well as in the future.

*In motivation:* the familiarity with models of motivation could cause Mr. Petheridge to review his attitude towards inter-branch and inter-bank competition. He could be encouraged to set targets for his staff to reach for and to give appropriate small rewards for success. He might also encourage staff, and trust them, to take a part in local events to enhance the name of the bank.

*In business development:* training in selling methods could lead to an improvement in branch performance, and even to that of Mr. Petheridge himself. To inform customers of useful new services, and have them avail themselves of the benefits thereof, need not be inconsistent with traditional service; and to approach the business community, including customers, in a systematic manner can still be done using the approach of the old-fashioned manager.

*iv.    The use of management-trained staff*

Judicious use of staff who are management-trained can release a good manager for higher-level duties. He can delegate organisational and administrative tasks; he can engage them in project work to do with branch development; he can use them for social or business purposes which their developed skills would equip them for. This would give him more time to devote to customer contact, and planning. If he were sensible he could even enlist their advice on a consultative basis in decisions affecting the branch's strategy so that he could benefit from a variety of ideas and stand a better chance of getting staff commitment.

Finally, he might like to consider what training he could do himself. Those who will claim that there is no substitute for experience will often add that it is never too late to learn!

If persuasion is successful, it would be helpful to the case of the two senior clerks if they have available all the necessary formalities in the way of forms and procedures for their own nomination: be they old-fashioned or modern, managers will only help those who help themselves ....

# CASE STUDY 9

Each quarter, the assistant personnel manager of one of the major clearing banks monitors the turnover of staff from the branches in the region for which he is responsible. At the last quarterly check he discovered that three members of staff from one branch have resigned in the period. Alerted to a possible problem, he checked over a longer period, and was perturbed to find that eleven other staff-members have resigned from this same branch in the previous twelve months.

Needless to say, this is a far higher number than one would expect and the assistant manager reported the figures to his senior colleagues. On their instigation he obtained further information about the branch and those who have resigned. The following brief facts emerge:

— All the leavers worked in the branch operations room and dealt with the processing of the daily vouchers through the branch terminal, and associated clerical duties.

— Nearly all were school leavers aged between 16 and 18 and had worked for the bank for an average of a year.

— The branch is an old-fashioned one both in the sense of its managerial style, which is of a formality suited to its city-centre customers, and in its building dating back to the last century.

— There are 100 staff at the branch, not many of whom have direct customer contact.

— The operations room has not, as far as can be determined from the files, had any change in supervision in the last 18 months.

The assistant personnel manager arranged to meet the branch management to investigate further and to examine the means of solving such problems as may be discovered.

1. Discuss in general terms the significance of high labour turnover.

2. Outline the process through which the assistant personnel manager should go to determine the possible causes of people leaving this particular branch.

3. Indicate some measures the branch management might take to alleviate those causes.

# CASE STUDY 9 — MODEL ANSWER

**The Problem**

High staff turnover can be costly, in the expenditure needed to recruit (advertising, recruitment administration and staffing, the time taken to interview by line-staff), to put people on the payroll (computer administration, tax and national insurance), to train them to appropriate levels of effectiveness. There are also the costs — the reverse of some of these — when people go.

It is also inconvenient and causes inefficiency as jobs are handed over from person to person and the smooth operation of the organisation is impaired. The application of this in a clearing bank is very clear.

*Labour turnover* statistics provide an organisation with information about the number of people who leave that organisation during a specific period.

These statistics help to give an insight into the effectiveness of recruitment and selection methods, training and development practices and the level of staff morale.

They also give a basis for ensuring that staffing levels are maintained not only at correct numbers but with a good mix of age, education and ability levels to ensure an adequate response to future needs.

**Analysis**

*Diagnosis* involves the investigation of the causes of the high leaving-rate. We do not know if the branch staff carried out exit interviews with the staff who are leaving. If so the file notes must be examined. In any case the investigation might look into some of the following:

(a) The job itself: is there a lack of variety in the work which makes it intolerably tedious?

Are there opportunities to progress to a higher level, or indeed to other tasks on the same level?

(b) Are the work conditions reasonable, and not physically uncomfortable: damp or cold or dark?

(c) Are the staff properly qualified for the tasks, neither under-qualified and finding them difficult, nor over-qualified and totally under-stretched?

(d)    Are there people in the situation who cause unrest: a core of settled employees who resent the intrusion of newcomers, or a supervisor who is difficult to work with?

(e)    Are there external factors affecting younger people at this branch, e.g. a new bank recruiting in the area, or recently developed transport problems?

**Solutions**    The bank management might wish to alleviate any immediate problems shown by the above investigation. However, the existence of a problem is not in doubt, and some of the following actions might be taken depending on the outcome of the diagnosis:

(a)    *Improve working conditions,* if necessary. Poor working conditions can be very discouraging to staff.

(b)    *Conduct exit interviews:* if these have not been done, then however embarrassing they may be (and it cannot be claimed that it is an easy task), management must attempt to find out why people leave. If branch management do not find they can do the interviews, personnel department should conduct them.

(c)    *Consider job-rotation,* which might alleviate the boredom of repetitive, simple tasks; within the operations room itself.

(d)    *Job-enrichment,* looking at the other side of Hertzberg's theory: can the clerks be given additional, interesting tasks, with responsibility attached and advancement possible in the context of the fresh work? Can they be formed into teams for the performing of more complex project-style operations?

(e)    *Recruitment procedure* should be monitored. Possibly the wrong type of staff are being recruited for this particular branch, and personnel department may wish to consult local management on this and seek their advice on future recruitment policy and practice.

(f)    *Compare, contrast and learn* from the experience of other branches of this size and type. Is the problem repeated elsewhere, and if so what have they done about it: if not have they somehow prevented it in ways we could use here?

(g)    The personnel department should maintain the contact with the branch to monitor future developments and take appropriate action.

# CASE STUDY 10

You are the assistant manager of your branch. You like talking to your staff and are sensitive to their problems. You are concerned about Kate Jones. Kate is 26 years old. She joined the bank at 16 with the minimum entry requirements, and surely and determinedly she has worked her way up to Grade 3 in your 20-strong branch. Kate is a quiet, mature woman, smart and attractive and reasonably sociable. She gets on well with the other members of staff, especially the younger ones, who invariably come to her with their technical and personal problems. She rarely talks about her own private life, about which little is known by her colleagues. In fact there is little to know, since she leads a fairly conventional life and is on good terms with her parents and her current boyfriend, about whom she is not particularly serious. She has three subjects left to complete her AIB, and until recently has been reasonably satisfied with her progress.

Her main job is securities. She handles all but the more complex securities for advances. She was looking forward to taking on more responsible securities work when Bill McCormack arrived to replace the Grade 4, Jack Cope, with whom Kate had got on very well. McCormack has been in the office for two months now.

Jack had trusted Kate, and allowed her to complete her work before checking it, which he always said he did "because I have to and not because I think I'll find any mistakes". He also gave Kate gradually more complex work so that she felt she was always learning something new.

McCormack immediately adopted a different line. He is younger than Kate by some six months, but is technically excellent, and is already an AIB. Since his arrival he has taken on all the complex securities work, and has even completed some of the work that Kate used to do, in order, he says, to familiarise himself with the customers. He is very sensitive about his responsiblility for what he has taken to calling "Securities Section" — you can hear the capital letters when he answers the telephone — and he stands over Kate, pointing out errors which she probably would have corrected herself and telling her how to perform tasks she already knows about. He lets her know in no uncertain terms that he feels responsible for all the work, including hers.

Kate eventually admitted to you that when McCormack arrived she resented it, thinking that maybe she could have managed the Grade 4 job herself. She is realistic enough, however, to acknowlege now that Bill is technically better suited to the work. However, she wants to progress at least to Grade 4 and possibly beyond, one day. Kate is now so clearly unhappy that the branch manager has asked you to look into it.

How would you define the problems involved in this situation, and how would you go about solving them?

# CASE STUDY 10 — MODEL ANSWER

**The Problem**   Kate Jones is unhappy, and by no means as productive as she can be. Her career has taken a setback and the path is blocked. However much she claims that she does not resent Bill McCormark's promotion, there must be some bitterness, she will find it hard to overcome. Furthermore, she is not trusted. On the positive side, she is receptive to responsibility and is prepared to be realistic about how she is to gain advancement.

Bill McCormack, though technically excellent, is inexperienced in management. He probably does not realise the effect that his attempts to establish himself as the securities expert is having on Kate, nor is he sensitive to her feelings about his appointment. He may, however, feel that because she is older than he is, and also because she is a women, he needs to exert his authority to prove their relative standing. On the positive side, he is energetic and enthusiastic and of undoubted expertise, and can be an asset to the branch.

Unless something is done, the work in the security section will deteriorate as Kate's morale drops, she continues to be inefficiently employed and as she leaves more and more to McCormack. In turn, he will trust her even less and assume an excessive load, grow to resent her and will delegate even less.

**Solutions**   The assistant manager must take the situation in hand, and may wish to do some of the following:

1.  Speak to McCormack and discuss:

    (a)   The way he allocates work. The advantages of delegation in order to make the most effective use of people and to help develop them.

    (b)   His reasons for wishing to establish himself. Praise the rise in the standards and status of the securities section, but get him to acknowledge the dangers of alienating the staff, especially Kate.

    (c)   His responsibility for training Kate for a more senior position in the future, either as he moves on or as she moves elsewhere; and as a back-up in his absence.

    (d)   Managerial support for decisions he makes provided that they are for the good of the whole branch and all the staff.

    (e)   Supervisory training now that he has the responsibility for the work of others.

2.   Speak to Kate and discuss:

    (a)   The nature of the relationship with McCormack and the need to find a mutually acceptable solution.

    (b)   Her attitude towards McCormack when he came; her current attitude; ways in which they can cooperate and work together for their mutual benefit.

    (c)   Formal training and courses she can attend to improve her technical knowledge in securities or her potential performance in other areas. Get her to develop with McCormack a programme of training and on-the-job development.

    (d)   Opportunities for development in another department in the medium term.

3.   Having McCormack schedule a programme of delegation and training for Kate, to be agreed with the assistant manager. Help McCormack to talk to Kate about their work relationship, openly and frankly.

4.   Make arrangements for formal training for both parties at an early stage.

5.   Monitor progress and keep an eye on developments. Keep personnel department informed of Kate's readiness for promotion, when appropriate. Consider both for management training if they show potential in this direction.

It would be mistaken to think that any or all of these suggestions will, either immediately or in the future, guarantee peace and harmony. However, this is the sort of motivational/conflict problem which, if no solution is applied, will undoubtedly deteriorate into a confrontation difficult to resolve.

The above suggestions depend on goodwill on all sides, and also a willingness to take a long-term view. The assistant manager must keep a constant eye on the situation and be ready to modify the action if it is not effective. One of the important things to note is that if this sort of situation is ignored, it will NOT go away.

# CASE STUDY 11

John Brown is chief clerk of University branch. He was recently given responsibility for organising a one-week student promotional campaign at the local university, to persuade as many students as possible to open accounts with the bank.

Before the campaign, Brown planned the tasks and the deployment of his team very carefully around the various parts of the university. However, due to the pressure of time, he could not arrange a briefing meeting with them until 4.45pm on the Friday before the promotion was due to start. While he recognised that this was not ideal, he felt that as most of the staff had worked on similar promotions in previous years a short meeting would suffice.

The staff were annoyed that he had left the meeting until so late, and some of the more senior people made it quite clear from their manner, their comments and glances at the clock that they wanted it over and done with as quickly as possible. Embarrassed by this, Brown hurried through the details of the allocation of tasks and how, when and where to perform them.

At five minutes past five, Brown asked if everyone understood what they had to do. This was seen as a cue for an immediate mass exodus through the door of the branch.

The campaign began at 9am the following Monday. Brown went to the campus late that afternoon to visit each of his team and to monitor progress. He was surprised to hear that it took some of his staff at least an hour to find their designated positions since they had not realised that the University had altered the location of some of the departments in the last twelve months.

He was even more upset to find that Mary, a 17 year old clerk, was not at the post assigned to her in the Dental School at all, to the delight of competitors who were engaged in similar campaigns. Nobody had seen her all day. He eventually found her near the staff lounge, lonely and disconsolate, having opened no accounts at all.

Brown was very annoyed. He angrily confronted Mary and asked her why she was not where she should be. In tears she replied that she had not understood what he had said at the meeting on Friday. She did not like to ask questions because everybody else seemed to know all about it and they all wanted to go home. She also confessed that she was frightened to tell him that she had not understood because he was known to be a very strict person and would be cross with her.

Brown had planned the campaign with care and in detail. His control mechanisms were efficient enough to pick up the problems early. However, due to a shortcoming in communication the promotion got off to a poor start, with valuable business lost. How could Brown have avoided the problem?

# CASE STUDY 11 — MODEL ANSWER

**Problem**  The ability to communicate is a vital management skill, as Brown's failure indicates. Without effective communication, coordination is frustrated and productivity diminished. To consider how Brown could have avoided the situation we must look initially at the barriers which prevented effective communication.

1.  The timing of the meeting did not encourage staff to be attentive or receptive, or willing to provide positive feedback in the form of questions or comments or suggestions.

2.  There was a strong non-verbal communication that the group wanted the meeting to end. Brown gave in to the feelings he sensed rather than confronting the staff.

3.  Group pressure inhibited people, especially very junior staff members from asking questions to clarify the briefing.

4.  Brown made an incorrect assumption in taking it for granted that all staff had sufficient previous knowledge and experience to handle the promotional campaign.

5.  Brown seems to have an authoritarian style which discouraged Mary from asking questions.

6.  Brown has depended on oral communication alone, which may have been insufficient in this case.

**Solutions**  1.  He could have prepared a written brief and circulated it to all concerned several days before the meeting. It would include:

   (a)  Details of the team members with each individual's task clearly defined.

   (b)  A brief set of reasons for each task.

   (c)  A map of the campus specifying the position of each team member.

   (d)  A general explanation of the importance of a successful student promotion to the bank.

(e)    A request for points, suggestions and questions to be raised either before or at the meeting.

(f)    The date and time of the final briefing meeting.

This would have given each team member the chance to study the operational details, both for themselves and the group. They would then be better able to raise questions and clarify misunderstandings and improve coordination by an understanding of each other's functions.

The written communication should, of course, be complete and accurate and yet as brief as possible, containing only information which is relevant and necessary. Jargon and technical phrases are quite unnecessary in this case.

2.    A staff meeting for a final briefing is still needed. To encourage receptivity and participation it should not be held before lunch or coffee breaks or in home time. The location should be secluded from distraction, and reasonably comfortable. If none of this is possible, the leader must acknowledge rather than try to ignore the clear, if non-verbally expressed, views of the team.

There should be a clear agenda and questions and points arising should be invited. Inexperienced members of the team should be encouraged to contribute, and their understanding checked by asking them to play back their view of what they have to do and how they have to do it. More experienced team members should be encouraged to share their knowledge with the others.

3.    Brown should be counselled on his style and the advantages of more participative styles should be discussed with him.

# CASE STUDY 12

You are the assistant manager of a small branch in a provincial town. Since the arrival of a new manager six months ago, a number of changes have been made in the branch organisational structure, because the manager wants to increase the volume of business and he intends to create a more effective unit to achieve it.

As a result of these changes two people of very different career ambitions and temperament have been brought together as working partners:

Margaret Brown is single, Grade 4, age 46 years. She has worked for the bank for over 30 years. She is methodical and accurate. She doesn't like the new working practices as she feels that her old method of working was always perfectly adequate to complete the work on time. She has not been considered for the bank's management training programme, and has said that she's perfectly happy where she is. She is popular with staff, customers and management.

Mark Fairhurst is Grade 3, single, aged 24 years. He entered the bank with 'A' levels. Until three months ago he was a clerk at the town's main branch. He recently obtained his AIB and has shown himself able and quick to learn. He is, sometimes, a little over-eager and frequently remarks how much more efficient the main branch is. His managers consider him a little immature, but he hopes to gain promotion and selection for the management training programme in the near future.

In the last fortnight you have detected undercurrents of dispute and discontent among the staff, and have overheard conversations which make it clear that Mark and Margaret are in direct conflict. You have heard them exchanging heated words. You are concerned that the problem might affect other staff and ultimately the smooth running of the branch.


Outline the main points of a plan to help resolve the problem, and explain the importance and relevance of each point.

# CASE STUDY 12 — MODEL ANSWER

**Problem**

There is evidence of an interpersonal problem between Margaret and Mark: rows and argument, rumour and conversations between others.

The causes must be investigated. It would be reasonable to assume that they may lie in differing backgrounds, ages, ambitions, motivations and different attitudes towards new working practices.

This makes it difficult for the two of them to understand each other and the difficulty must be resolved before it lowers staff morale and impedes customer service.

*Options:*

(a)   The branch organisation could be altered to separate the work of Mark and Margaret; but this might only result in a short-term solution in such a small branch where at some time they will have to cooperate in one way or another.

(b)   A transfer to another branch might be arranged for one or the other. But Mark has just arrived, and until recently Margaret has been happy here. She would certainly not wish to be moved just because of her problems with Mark; and such a move is never administratively simple.

(c)   Alternatively a plan could be worked out to overcome the intransigence of both parties to enable them to come to terms with working well together.

**Solutions**

1.   Arrange a meeting between the three of you in your office. Privacy is essential for frankness and to encourage openness.

2.   Start by speaking concisely about what has come to your attention:

— particular incidents of dispute

— the conversations of others

— the seriousness of the problem (not just to themselves)

— the need for a solution beneficial to them and the branch.

3. Set out some rules for procedure:

   — Each person will be allowed to talk uninterruptedly about how they see the situation.
   — Frankness will be essential, since you assume that each person wants to resolve the problem.
   — Confidentiality will be guaranteed.

These measures will give you the information you need to take the matter further. It is possible that neither party has been able, before now, to express their feelings and this in itself may contribute to a solution. No interruptions will be allowed because otherwise the battlefield is simply transferred to your office. Confidentiality proves your personal determination to solve the problem in your own domain, and the atmosphere of trust will help in the frankness of expression.

4. Listen carefully. Encourage them to expand on the points they make, but do not interrupt to make points or to say anything which may imply that you are taking sides. Take brief notes, if necessary.

The need for your attention is so that you can confirm earlier assumptions about the causes of the problems. You may discover new information. Furthermore, listening indicates your mature concern for the problem.

5. Obtain their suggestions for a solution to the problem of conflict. Exclude those which involve moves or transfers or alteration of duties which would imply avoidance rather than solution.

Any solution has to have their commitment, otherwise it will not work. If they can agree between themselves ways in which they can work together, this would be ideal. All that would then remain would be to ensure that the plans are carried out.

6.  Add your own suggestions, if they are not included in the plans put forward by the clerks. These might include:

— Margaret should consider adopting some of Mark's more sensible suggestions concerning modern work-practices.

— Mark should learn traditional routines where beneficial, and not advocate change for change's sake.

— Conflict should be resolved maturely and openly between them.

— They should plan to divide the work to take advantage of their mutual strengths.

— Each should defer to the expertise of the other where appropriate.

— Each should allow for the different age and career aspirations of the other.

You may add other suggestions, but they should be in the interest of fulfilling the separate but cooperative needs of the individuals involved and the objectives of the branch management.

7.  Review the situation regularly and have follow-up discussions. Make it clear that you are going to do this and that you are determined not to allow the problem to recur.

# CASE STUDY 13

The administration department of the Northern Division of the bank has for many years operated with a secretarial staff of seven: a senior secretary working exclusively for the departmental manager, and the others in groups of two attached to each of three sections.

It was recently decided at senior level to reorganise the secretarial support by setting up a typing pool, in which all the secretaries work together instead of, as at present, in different locations. It had been calculated that pooling in this way, together with the introduction of three word-processors, would allow the department to operate on a reduced level of five secretarial staff. The reduction in numbers would come about by natural wastage, since two of the secretaries reach retirement age within twelve months.

The task of reorganisation was given to John Taylor, seconded in for three months from a local branch. This move was not welcomed by the Departmental Manager: Taylor was known to be somewhat secretive and arrogant; the manager was not consulted about Taylor, who was in any case an "outsider"; and the manager did not like the idea of losing his personal secretary, Joan Newhurst, whom he told about the plans.

She in turn feared the loss of her seniority, and lost no time in telling her colleagues, emphasising the introduction of these "infernal machines" which were intended to take away their jobs. In no time, the rumour spread of redundancies which would result from new technology which the secretaries would be forced to adopt. When Joan confronted Taylor, he made matters worse. He was not yet ready to make any announcements and he abruptly dismissed her enquiry, telling her that if there were any information to give to the secretaries he would do that when he felt the time was right.

Some three weeks later Taylor announced the plans. Although the terms and timing of the changes were considerably more favourable than the secretaries had expected, the suspicions which had been built up by that time were so great that the plans were implemented only with great reluctance. Some teething troubles were encountered, and there were no evident attempts to solve them, although a little initiative could have done so. The quality of the work was at the minimum required, although the previous standard had been exceptionally high; and a certain wry satisfaction was evident in almost all the girls every time the plans hit a snag.

As Joan pointed out to Taylor, "None of this would have happened if you'd told us all about it earlier". The standard of work is now high. Morale is beginning to rise again under the new system; and the scheme is now to be adopted in Southern Division.

Assess the shortcomings in the way in which the changes were handled by the bank. How can the problems be avoided in Southern Division?

# CASE STUDY 13 — MODEL ANSWER

**Problem**      —  Decisions were taken at all levels without consultation, resulting in lower efficiency, lower morale and cooperation.

      — Management failed to learn from past experience in the introduction of new technology, causing fear and concern among the target staff, who were not even consulted.

      — Communication was poorly handled. Information about the new scheme was leaked and disseminated by those with a hostile viewpoint who gave a distorted account of possible outcomes.

      — The manager's commitment was at best uncertain, and senior people had failed to enlist his support. The result was that he did not give constructive help to Taylor, the consultant.

      — The combination of outsider status and an abrasive personality made the consultant less effective than he might have been. His actions in the early part of the episode would have added a measure of mistrust to those problems.

In summary, there was a failure to anticipate problems in the plans for change, a failure to consult with the staff; and poor communication by the consultant.

**Solutions**     Southern Division may like to introduce the changes as follows:

1. The senior manager should consult the departmental manager immediately. The latter will lose his personal secretary but will be shown the benefits to the bank and the department. He will also be involved in the choice of consultant.

2. The departmental manager will cooperate with the consultant. An early preliminary announcement will be made to the secretaries to allay insecurity and to emphasise the intention to communicate frequently and openly.

3.  The consultant should talk as early as possible to the senior secretary, and then the others. Initial discussions must include assurances about the absence of enforced redundancies; the provision of training for new technology; no loss of job seniority; and the benefits to the department of the new scheme.

4.  The secretaries must be encouraged to make suggestions to help plan and implement the scheme. Personal preferences may be accommodated in the matter of location or colleague relationships where possible. Familiarisation with word-processors before the formal training will be encouraged, if such machines are operated in other parts of the bank and are available for experimentation, on the initiative of the secretaries.

**A Note on Leadership Styles**

A consultative approach to change is not without possible problems. Early information about changes can allow opposition to develop, strengthen and grow. The less palatable aspects of the changes can take on a disproportionate importance and outweigh the advantages in the minds of the staff involved. The timing can be problematic if start dates have to be postponed and waiting time lengthened so that anxieties might develop. If an excessive amount of work is demanded to help in the formation and implementation of the plans, resentment as to the proper work of management and staff can occur.

On the other hand, it is absolutely vital to the success of the scheme that the cooperation of the manager and the secretaries is obtained. The promise of information, consultation and a thorough discussion of problems is likely to produce better results.

# CASE STUDY 14

The shopping centre branch of a well-known bank is housed in a modern, air conditioned building situated in a prime location in the town. It has its full complement of staff, who are well-trained; but contrary to expectation, it seems to have been losing business to other banks and failing to meet targets. When it was reported to the regional manager that two staff had asked for transfers, he called in on the manager.

At the interview it was revealed that friction had arisen between the manager and his senior assistant, John Hardman, and between John and staff. According to the manager, John Hardman had an abrasive personality which showed through in his management style. He was authoritarian and domineering in his dealings with the staff, and contemptuous of their intellect: "half-wits" was a word he used frequently, although the manager had pointed out that more than one had achieved good 'A' level grades and had still chosen to work for the bank rather than go to university.

The manager admitted that he found the strain of working with Hardman very wearing himself. In spite of several "quiet words" with him, John had not altered his behaviour and the manager had been forced into the role of peacemaker to ensure a semblance of good relations in the branch.

He added that the staff no longer seem to want to do things when asked. They display a surly attitude towards customers, and they are no longer prepared to work beyond normal hours, except under extreme pressure. This pressure usually takes the form of threatening behaviour from Hardman who says that the only important thing is to get the work out by the end of the day. It is established that the branch problems actually began nine months ago when Hardman arrived.

The regional manager decided to talk to Hardman himself. It transpired that Hardman had been brought up, and had also been first employed, in a depressed and tough area of the city. He had had a weak boss who never gave the staff any direction, which resulted in an easygoing attitude and an unacceptable slackness, which Hardman wanted never to repeat when he obtained a managerial post.

For this reason Hardman supervises the work very closely. He doesn't listen to suggestions; he prefers the staff simply to do the work his way. He likes them to stick to their technical tasks and leave the managerial work to him. He has been known to struggle with a problem for days, when, if he asked one of his clerks, it could be solved in minutes.


Explain and discuss Hardman's management style. Make suggestions as to how the situation at Shopping Centre branch could be improved.

# CASE STUDY 14 — MODEL ANSWER

**The Problem**  Hardman is very autocratic. He gives orders and expects them to be obeyed. He does not encourage his staff to produce ideas to improve the branch. He just expects them to get on with their technical task. The result is that they are unhappy, resentful and uncooperative. As a consequence their service declines and the branch loses business. To reverse the situation, Hardman must be persuaded to involve staff more in his decisions by telling them what is going on, getting their ideas for improvement and making decisions which reflect the useful and practical suggestions which emerge.

**Solutions**  To alter a manager's management style is not a simple task and will take considerable time and effort.

His manager should explain to Hardman that many benefits are likely to arise which would increase the effectiveness of the branch, if staff were given a greater opportunity to participate more actively in the work and were encouraged to make suggestions about improving the quality and range of services it offers.

The manager should develop an action plan with Hardman. This would involve:

A clear definition formulated between the manager and Hardman of the latter's responsibilities.

A programme of careful delegation from Hardman to senior clerical staff, of supervisory responsibilities.

A system to encourage suggestions from staff about such topics as branch appearance or customer service.

The production of an action plan for business development, which would draw on the knowledge, skill and expertise of all staff.

Regular discussion between the manager and Hardman on his progress.

Formal management training using the bank's training department's facilities.

**Follow-up**

The regional manager should monitor the situation, ensuring that Hardman does improve. If not, Hardman's future will have to be reassessed.

He will also make sure that the manager firmly pursues the programme for Hardman's development and does not let up.

The decline in business must be halted, and reversed, and the regional manager will have to keep a close eye on the progresss of the branch.

Finally, staff morale must be monitored through factors like labour turnover, absenteeism, productivity levels and requests for transfer.

# CASE STUDY 15

You have recently been appointed assistant manager in a small branch with a staff of 13, and it is one of your prime objectives to develop a highly motivated, achievement-oriented team under your leadership. Fortunately, your predecessor had performed well and the staff are largely committed and enthusiastic. On your arrival, however, you have observed that one individual, Edward Clark, does not seem to be working to what you and your manager perceive to be his full potential despite adequate training and experience.

Clark is 49 years of age. He joined the bank in 1969 from an insurance company at a time when it was difficult to recruit good staff as school leavers. He took clerical jobs at several branches, and learnt the technical aspects of his job quite well. His work is still technically adequate; but he has had no advancement in Grade since he completed his initial training.

The main reason for this is that he is basically lazy, and avoids work and responsibility. On more than one occasion he has been threatened with disciplinary action, but he has avoided real punishment by working harder during the period he was on trial. As the crisis faded, however, he has always reverted to his old ways.

At present he is working as a filing clerk, which suits him, because he spends most of his time on his own, subject to very little supervision, and can go at his own pace, and also avoid the customers who invariably (he says) just create extra work for him. It also suits the manager, who thinks that Clark has a demoralising effect on others in the branch. He has more or less given up on Clark after many attempts to improve his performance.

Recently Clark's work has again deteriorated to an unacceptable level. Items are incorrectly filed, his work area is intolerably untidy, he has made mistakes which other staff have had to correct and they have had to help him to complete his tasks. Indeed he is now at the stage where a part-timer would be able to do his job and have time to spare.

Your enquiries have revealed that both manager and staff believe that Clark has the potential to do a good job at clerical level, and is quite capable of handling work at a more senior level if he wanted to and if he could summon the energy. As it is, the effect he is having on the branch is at best neutral, at worst negative.

How can you approach the problem of Clark's performance in the context of your overall objectives for the branch?

# CASE STUDY 15 — MODEL ANSWER

**Problem**

Clark's work has deteriorated; his work area is untidy; items are incorrectly filed; he is making mistakes which have to be corrected by other members of staff.

Clark is lazy and unmotivated. He works under little or no supervision. The manager devotes little or no effort to help or correct the situation; and no previous "treatment" has had any effect. He clearly derives little or no satisfaction from his job, which is merely a means to an end. He appears to come to work to satisfy what Maslow terms Primary Needs (physiological and safety). He feels no need to belong to a group, or to distinguish himself as an individual. It is difficult to see how to motivate him.

**Solutions**

The following factors influence the nature of the solution:

(a)  The bank's disciplinary system is less than effective with a person who is capable of bursts of energy to boost his performance to acceptable levels.

(b)  Having been so long in one grade, Clark will be at the maximum salary level and threats of future withholding of increments are not relevant.

(c)  Clark's personality and history indicate little hope for solutions involving positive reward, of the type involving the promise of responsibility or advancement.

(d)  However, even Clark comes to work to fulfil needs, and a measure of effective performance, however limited, can be obtained from him if it is indicated that his behaviour threatens the satisfaction of those needs.

His manager must also exercise more control and monitor Clark's progress very carefully.

—  The job he does should be analysed in detail and realistic short-term goals should be set for him

—  These goals and his progress towards them should be monitored frequently.

—  Clark should be given feedback frequently i.e. weekly or even daily.

—  He should be given coaching, counselling and training to help him improve.

—   His needs for food, warmth, shelter and safety and security should be used: it must be pointed out that these are satisfied by his continued employment, which is now under threat.

—   Clark should also be encouraged when his performance is acceptable to reinforce proper behaviour.

—   If he does not improve he should be taken through the warning system and dismissed.

Positive motivation does not in every case work; here the combination negative reinforcement, control and warning may produce sufficient improvement to make Clark give an acceptable performance.

# CASE STUDY 16

You are the assistant manager of your branch, which comprises in addition to yourself and the manager, ten clerks. It is a well organised and efficient branch. Staff morale is high, and you and the manager pride yourselves on having built a good team.

Three months ago you were selected as the branch to be responsible for the first half-year training of a new graduate entrant, Tim Whittaker, prior to his moving to a larger branch as part of his two-year accelerated induction programme. He would be the first graduate you had taken in this way; and his open, friendly manner made him generally acceptable to all.

As the weeks progressed, however, it became increasingly apparent to you that feelings of resentment were developing, especially among those the same age as Tim, over his particularly rapid advancement through the clerical jobs. Several juniors voiced the opinion, to you as well as to each other, that Tim was allowed to attend training courses that they had never been on, and that he could move on to new jobs when hardly proficient in the previous one, which was more than they could do even after months on the job. All of this is substantially true, and you have every sympathy with the views expressed; but you also have training responsibility for Tim, who is aware of the feelings, having overheard the comments on more than one occasion.

Tim Whittaker is not blameless. He frequently wanders about the office saying he is bored, which simply rubs salt in the wound. Moreover, he is not above using his intellectual and verbal skills to intimidate other members of staff, for instance at staff meetings, by employing purely destructive, clever criticism.

You have also observed that he does not principally identify himself as a member of the branch but rather as a 'graduate trainee' with more in common with others on the graduate training programme (whom he meets weekly at college during his Institute studies and on training courses) than with his colleagues at the branch.

To emphasise this, he recently chose to spend the weekend with his graduate friends in London rather than join the staff on a branch outing to a local agricultural show where the bank's mobile branch formed the centrepiece of a very pleasant afternoon. Tim was the only branch member not to turn up.

He has three more months to work with you. In that time, how will you endeavour to reconcile the needs of your graduate trainee with those of your regular staff, and make him a more acceptable and useful team member?

PATRONISING TO
THE N$^{\text{TH}}$ DEGREE

# CASE STUDY 16 — MODEL ANSWER

**Problem**

Tim says he is bored; staff are openly unhappy about his comparative progress; Tim is making his intellectual strength known in a negative manner; he is clearly not identifying himself as a member of the branch, but as a member of another group. This can lead to lower morale and performance, to less good work from Tim, and to less than effective training experiences for Tim if he is exluded from the groups from whom he is expected to learn.

The staff form a primary group: all twelve in close day-to-day work contact. Each has a clearly defined role. They know of, and have a positive attitude to, the roles of others. The group has a set of norms accepted by all, and a set of standards of behaviour. They form a very stable team.

Normally they are able to identify and accept the role of a new person entering the group from outside, provided that the person fits with the group and accepts their norms.

In some ways Tim did this at first: he accepted his learning role, as any newcomer would, and he was friendly and open — again, acceptable normal behaviour.

However, he has recently behaved less acceptably and has been treated with less consideration as a result. His training cuts across accepted hierarchical patterns, time-programmes, and established norms concerning the establishment of proficiency in one task before attempting (or being allowed to attempt) the next.

His own behaviour exacerbates the situation. He detaches himself by his claim to be bored, and by his clever criticisms. He seems to think that he is of a different order of person. He openly indicates his preference for membership of a different group, that of the graduates; and he emphasises this by choosing to attend their social function.

The manager must (a) maintain the current performance and morale of the group, under threat from a disruptive influence; (b) maintain Tim's own performance and morale by providing good training for him; (c) establish his ability to train graduates as a contribution to the bank's training programme.

**Solutions**      Any solution must take into account frustrated expectations on both sides: those of the staff who accepted an unusual new entrant, and those of Tim in wanting to make fast progress. It is not open to the manager to remove or transfer Tim: the bank relies on him to train Tim, who is no better or worse than other new entrants with special training requirements. The following approach might be made:

1.   Take the complaints of the current staff very seriously. Take time to explain the need for multi-tier entry and the special needs and abilities of the degree-trained person. Explain the full accelerated graduate programme.

2.   Make this an opportunity to re-examine the career progress of current staff members and review the branch training schedule. Plan for training courses for all who need them.

3.   Look afresh at whatever is planned for Tim while at the branch. Is he spending long enough on each function? Are you concentrating on his learning as well as the timing of his moves?

4.   Give him an interim appraisal. As Tim is inexperienced in the work of the branch and needs to learn how to deal with people of a different educational background, Tim has a great deal to learn about life at branch level.

5.   Advise Tim on specific aspects of his behaviour. Brief him to be positive and supportive in branch meetings, using his undoubted intellectual ability to build on the ideas of his colleagues. Ask him to make efforts to join social activities, at the branch.

6.   Set him specific behavioural goals and counsel him regularly on his progress.

7.   See to it that both permanent staff and Tim perceive the value of cooperation for the sake of the branch and the bank by ensuring that they work consciously towards group goals. Give them all feedback on any behaviour which is likely to affect performance adversely.

# CASE STUDY 17

In your office a problem has recently arisen concerning the performance of Sandie Swallow. It's not that she is failing to complete the work, although there is a danger of that. She is only just keeping up. The real problem is her timekeeping.

Every morning, it seems, with but a few exceptions, Sandie turns up late, looking tired and dishevelled as though she has had too little sleep. There is always a childish excuse:- the alarm-clock failed to go off, the train mysteriously left the station five minutes early and she missed it; she had to go back for her sandwiches, and so on. Few of these excuses ring true, and the poor timekeeping is such that now something will have to be done about it.

Sandie is nineteen years old, slim and extremely pretty but she does not flaunt her attractiveness. At her best she is very competent at her work and she often makes intelligent contributions to discussions on improving work practices. She used to make no secret of her ambitions for her career. She wanted to be a branch manager by the age of 35. Coinciding with the deterioration in her ability to get to work on time, she has stopped talking about progress towards her ambition.

A week or two ago the assistant manager took Sandie to task about her lateness. She muttered something about being very tired, because of studying twice weekly at the local college for her AIB, and the workload in preparation, essays and reading. He promised to give her any help he could, but warned her to organise herself better to get to work on time.

Sandie's section leader has become more and more exasperated with her; and this morning at about 09.45, everyone was horrified to hear him completely blow his top with her, in the hearing of all including the assistant manager.

"So, you've finally turned up", he said loudly. "I hope the 'gig' went all right. I wish you'd make your mind up about your career, young lady. Are you going to sing full-time with your brother's group, or settle down to a proper job in the bank? I'm fed up with us having to suffer from you singing in clubs till heaven knows what hour every night, then staggering in here an hour late every morning. You'd better decide quickly or you're for it."

Comment on this situation. If you were the assistant manager, what steps would you now take to resolve it?

# CASE STUDY 17 — MODEL ANSWER

**Problem**    There are four related problems the assistant manager must face:

1. Sandie's bad timekeeping.
2. The fact that Sandie has lied to him about the root cause of the lateness.
3. Sandie's career conflict between pop-singing and banking.
4. The manner in which the section leader has dealt with the problem including this morning's incident.

Sandie has evidently been singing with the band, and getting insufficient sleep to allow her to arrive on time to work effectively in the branch.

She is torn between success in the music world and her career in the bank. She has not felt able to tell the bank management of this, in fact she has lied to her assistant manager both about her tiredness and the reasons for her bad timekeeping.

While the Section Leader's exasperation is understandable, his behaviour in reprimanding Sandie in front of all who may hear is not only inconsiderate but unlikely to have the desired effect and is not sound management practice.

These are urgent matters and the assistant manager must take immediate steps to resolve the situation. Some of the following might be advisable:

**Solutions**    Since the section leader seems to know something of the case, and because it would otherwise seem to be by-passing him, the assistant manager should tell Sandie that he will want to speak to her soon but should first talk to the section leader privately.

In this conversation the assistant manager should

Establish what facts the section leader has concerning the involvement of Sandie in the band.

— Check his opinion of how serious she is about having to choose between one career and the other.

— Establish precisely the record of the incidence of Sandie's lateness over the last few weeks, and her given reasons.

— Allow the section leader to speak about his feelings concerning the problems caused by Sandie's behaviour, and about the incident of this morning.

— Point out that it is usually preferable to call subordinates aside to apply discipline, rather than do it publicly, since the humiliation added to the discipline does not usually help to improve performance.

— Indicate that what will be said to Sandie will be in support of the section leader's attitude, but that it must now be tackled by the assistant manager because of the inaccurate excuses made to him previously

The assistant manager must now rationally and calmly approach the problems of Sandie. He should prepare carefully to speak to her, specifying to himself some *objectives:*

1. To establish the truth of the situation.

2. To help Sandie clarify her own position so as to make sensible choices.

3. To ensure that, whatever those choices eventually are, Sandie does her work to the required standard meanwhile.

During his interview with Sandie he would:

1. Ask her to explain the exact situation concerning the band and her involvement.

2. Ask her to talk about her current attitude towards her banking career.

3. Indicate his disapproval because she lied on the previous occasion, but indicate his willingness to help her in her decisions now.

4. Point out some of the advantages in a banking career, in terms of advancement, security, interest and complexity, responsibility, personal growth and fulfilment. Point out some of the disadvantages of a career in popular music.

5. Tell her that good timekeeping and sufficient energy to fulfil her tasks are vital. Tell her she will be monitored carefully and subject to discipline if there is no improvement.

6. Agree with her a precise time to make her mind up about what she intends to do and a date to contact the assistant manager about her decisions.

**Follow-up**    Keep close contact with the section leader, having briefed him
to monitor Sandie's timekeeping and performance. Discuss
Sandie's views with her from time to time. Observe her
progress and encourage advances in her banking skills and
knowledge. Take firm action, once she has taken the decision
about her future.

# CASE STUDY 18

Derek Land is the head of a securities department in a large branch of a major clearing bank. He has a staff of seven, comprising an assistant manager, three senior and three junior clerks.

The department deals with the preparation of all items of corporate and personal security for the branch, other than those undertaken by solicitors, and it also provides and documents safe-custody facilities for customers, as well as dealing with stock exchange transactions for them. One of the features of work in the department is a considerable degree of liaison between the staff and outside bodies, including bank staff, customers, solicitors and stockbrokers.

Land was told that a graduate trainee would be joining the department in a fortnight's time, for a six-month period. Land's superiors did not know what the requirements were for this six months, and left it to Land to sort the matter out.

Since he had no experience of training graduates, and nor had any member of his department, Land telephoned the Graduate Liaison Officer for guidance. He was told that the graduate must acquire a good practical knowledge of securities work up to senior clerical level so that she may be transferred fully trained into a senior clerical position, since this particular young lady is nearing the end of her training period. She has had some branch clerical experience and has attended the bank's introductory securities course. She has as yet had no practical experience in securities.

She is already booked on to the intermediate securities course in about two months; and a further few months after that she would normally go on to the advanced securities course, though that would depend on branch recommendation. Other than these there are no formal arrangements and Land had a free hand in departmental training.

When she arrived, Virginia Knowles introduced herself, and Land called her in to his office to give her the information outlined above. To his amazement, this opened a floodgate of rage from Virginia:

"You mean there's hardly anything planned again? For 18 months this has happened to me — I always seem to come as a surprise. Nobody ever thinks of training in advance; I'm always a damned afterthought!" With some effort, Land was able to calm her down, and to assure her that, whatever her experiences had been so far, he would personally ensure effective planned training in the department.

How should he go about this task?

# CASE STUDY 18 — MODEL ANSWER

**Problem**   Land has no experience in training graduates, and has very little information on how to go about it. He has some minimal guidelines, and it is clear that the newcomer has to learn a job in a far shorter period than is usual. He has no information about the graduate and while he has a general idea of deadlines and fixed dates, these are not specific. Miss Knowles has obviously been dissatisfied with her training to date; Land is nevertheless required to establish a sensible programme, for his own sake, for that of the graduate, and for his department. He would therefore be well advised to approach the task in a systematic manner.

**Actions**   1.   Establish a set of training objectives

Land should estimate the level of competence to which the graduate must aspire, and put this into operational terms: he should be thinking in terms of how one might test that competence at the end of the period, broken down into headings and sub-headings of the skills and knowledge needed.

2.   Establish deadline dates

There are certain fixed events, such as the two courses and the end-dates, into which any practical plan must fit.

3.   Design a training plan

This will closely follow outlines suggested by the objectives and will develop skills and knowledge in a logical and staged manner. It should be done in association with the assistant manager, who should be entrusted with a good measure of responsibility for its progress.

4.   Establish a monitoring programme

Land must check at regular, planned stages the progress of the graduate towards her competence goals.

5.   Ensure that staff are clearly aware of their specific tasks in the training programme

Virginia will receive training from certain members of staff in the department at various stages of her programme. Those concerned should feel involved, and be quite clear as to their role. It is naturally vital that each person involved is competent at their own tasks.

**Advantages of a** — Fixes the field to be covered
**formal**         — Establishes the time scale (with some flexibility)
**programme**      — Forms a clear communication of responsibility to those
                     involved, ensuring smooth progress
                   — Permits candidate to monitor own progress
                   — Allows for a balance between theory and practice
                   — Motivates staff performing the training via their clearly
                     recognised involvement.

**Limitations**    — Could be rigid, and could (because of administrative
                     convenience) not permit useful variation
                   — Trainee might be unable to meet requirements at certain
                     stages, disrupting the rest
                   — Any lapse in the progress could cause friction in the
                     disturbance of the plans of staff members involved in the
                     training programme.
                   — Trained staff might nevertheless have unusual or
                     incorrect practices which may be passed on
                   — The burden of training could be onerous and cause
                     friction and ill-feeling; as could the clear sight of
                     accelerated training for a priviledged staff-member.

These limitations should be enumerated and foreseen.
Managerial behaviour on Land's part, and vigilance during
the course of the training, will alleviate them.

**Follow-up**   While the graduate's future training will not be Land's
responsibility, he will wish to record, possibly by file-note, the
progress at each stage of training, and will wish to make a final
report at the end.

He should obtain written feedback, as well as informal
opinions, from the graduate so as to improve performance,
if necessary, on the next occasion he must train someone.

He may also like to remind himself in his diary that he
should speak to the manager who will take the graduate on to
the staff, at some suitable future date, to assess the effectiveness of the training in use.

Finally he may wish to approach the Graduate Liaison
Officer to relay discreetly Miss Knowles' comments about her
training prior to arrival at the department, to permit the
Officer to investigate the matter.

# CASE STUDY 19

Rachel Walker has recently been transferred into her bank's personnel department at a level senior enough for her to take immediate responsibility for the recuitment of clerks for a region of the bank.

Since she has never done recruitment interviews before, she asked for advice from her colleague Anne, an experienced member of Personnel staff. She wanted guidance on the sort of questions she should ask to obtain information from the candidates.

Anne had a programme of interviews set for that day, and she said "Don't worry — there's nothing to interviewing and you're a natural, I can tell. Anyway, it's all a matter of common sense. Sit in with me a few times today, and you'll learn all there is to know."

Rachel sat in on the interviews and she was very impressed with the way Anne went through them in a polished and efficient manner. Because she was so new, however, Rachel emerged feeling little better equipped to do her own interviews, and still rather at a loss to know how to prepare properly for them. The following week, Rachel was plunged in at the deep end when, because of personnel department staff shortages, and a sudden heavy recruiting period, she was asked to conduct five interviews in a day, to recruit Grade 1 clerks from a selection of school-leavers.

She emerged, close to tears, at the end of the day. "I've no idea whether I've made the right decisions" she said to Anne: "I couldn't get them to talk; I'm sure I've given most of them the wrong end of the stick, and I really don't know what I'm doing. I need solid advice — I need to see more of your interviews, and I need TRAINING! I'll never be able to do this job properly and I'm supposed to do some more next week!"

Anne calmed her down and reassured her; and that evening determined to give thought to helping Rachel more systematically during the next day or two, by letting her sit in, by arranging a training schedule, and by giving her some methodical short-term advice.

Under these headings, then, if you were Anne,

(a) How would you describe the advantages and disadvantages of learning the techniques of interviewing by example?

b) Briefly describe how you would train Rachel properly for the job of recruitment interviewing.

(c) What short-term advice would you give so that Rachel can prepare to perform more effectively next week?

# CASE STUDY 19 — MODEL ANSWER

**Problem**  Rachel is unprepared to perform the task of recruitment interviewing well: she has no experience and she has not been trained. Personnel is a very high-cost item for an organisation and effective selection is very important.

Learning by example can be effective, but it needs preparation, or else the lessons will not be learnt or will soon be forgotten; and Rachel's first experience of "sitting in" was not effective. She needs to watch Anne again, this time better prepared with ideas of the advantages and disadvantages of learning this way: she needs proper longer-term training; and she needs advice on interviewing to prepare her for next week.

**Learning by example**  Advantages: Observation of experienced interviewers opening behaviour: putting the interviewee at ease

Observation of the forms of question, those which succeed and those which fail in gaining information

Observation of behaviours which are well received and cause the candidate to respond freely

Methods of note-taking and remembering the main points of the interview for later reference

The encouragement of the candidate to ask questions and the giving of bank information

The close of the interview and ways of leaving the candidate with a good impression of the bank.

Drawbacks: Difficulty in judging what is good and what is less effective behaviour on the part of the interviewer.

Narrow range of behaviours displayed by one single example

The acceptance (for want of developed critical faculties) of patently ineffective behaviour

Inability to reproduce behaviours which are related to the personality of the example-interviewer

Possible inability in debrief discussion of the example-interviewer to break-down and rationalise own behaviour. Possibly no theoretical base for it.

**Training**

Recruitment interviewing requires a set of professional interactive skills, and Rachel must be properly trained. Each bank approaches this in different ways, but among the training devices possible are the following:

— Formal training:

Internal personnel management courses

External courses

Management training courses with an element of interpersonal skills training.

— Specially designed training for Rachel and anyone else new in the department: designed on request from personnel with the close cooperation of Bank Training Department.

— Professional qualification: If Rachel eventually decides on a career in personnel, the Institute of Personnel Management have professional training for their qualification, often offered at local colleges or polytechnics.

— Reading: There are plenty of good books on personnel topics in general, and interviewing and recruitment in particular to which Rachel could be directed.

— Experience/observation: Provided that it is planned and monitored, with time set aside for overt review, sitting-in on Anne's interviews, and discussing the process involved in her own, should form part of the programme.

**Selection interviewing:**

Advice

— Obtain a clear job-description and a personnel specification

— Have a clear set of objectives for the interview itself

— Read the application forms carefully and seek points of interest to raise with the candidate

- Have all necessary information about the bank handy
- Prepare open-ended questions (What, how, why, tell me about...) and not those which require yes-or-no answers
- Ensure that the interview room is tidy and cheerful
- Ensure that there will be no interruptions
- Except in so far as they are indicated on the application form, seek information on factors in the Plan (five-point or seven-point) favoured by the bank, e.g. personal appearance, intellectual ability, home circumstances.
- Plan both the opening statement (brief, followed by an early, easy question) and the close (friendly but definite, and referring to the next action on the part of the bank)
- Take time after each interview to reflect on the candidate and his/her suitability, checking for correspondence with the job description, and against any personal prejudice on your part.
- Remember that the interview is a two-way selection process and you should try to represent the bank in its best light
- Make your decisions and communicate them clearly to those who must undertake the administration.

# CASE STUDY 20

One of the administrative departments of the Training Centre has just had the good fortune to obtain new office space, and Barbara, the administrative officer, is now faced with a difficult decision.

The new accommodation is at present a large open space, and it is to house three people: Margaret, who is of official rank and is a meticulous and efficient worker. (She is responsible for the work of the other two and usually supervises them quite closely); Denise, a mature and diligent senior clerk, who does most of the typing and high-level administrative work: and Jane, whose job includes a good deal of contact with trainees, and who acts as receptionist as well as handling the day-to-day paper work concerned with the finances of the Centre.

At the moment, all three staff occupy a fairly cramped single office. Mr Wallace, the training manager, has told Barbara that she can arrange for the division of the new office space in any way she likes: a small office for Margaret and a larger one for Denise and Jane, or three offices, one for each; or a single space as at present.

Barbara is an intelligent and logical person, and would like to come up with a solution to this problem which would suit the needs of the staff and of the department. Because of her contact with the staff in the past, she knows that there are no insurmountable personality clashes between any of the people involved other than minor irritations, some caused by the present lack of adequate space.

On the other hand, Barbara knows the ladies to be strong personalities, who will express their views on most topics, and will certainly have their own ideas about what they expect and hope for in the new accommodation. Furthermore, she knows Mr Wallace very well: a sympathetic but a critical character, who will inevitably question her closely on the process of decision-making through which she will go to arrive at her recommendations.

Without specifying what you would recommend as the final outcome, suggest the stages through which Barbara should go, illustrating each by examples from the case, to arrive at a decision and to implement it.

# CASE STUDY 20 — MODEL ANSWER

**Problem**    Barbara is in a classic decision-making situation. The objectives can be specified and it is clear that a decision cannot be avoided. There are benefits and drawbacks to each of several courses of action, and there is a fair amount of information available, but not all. There are personal as well as logical considerations, and opinions of those involved are germane to the decision.

**Suggested action—**    Specify the decision situation:
Barbara should take time to clarify in her mind the objectives to be achieved by a decision in this matter.

— Set criteria for a successful decision:
What would be a *good* decision in this case? Probably one which would ensure efficient working by each individual staff member; good communications between them; one which the girls themselves will accept happily.

— Obtain all available facts:
The costs of various alternatives, and the physical possibilities of dividing the space; opinions from the people involved, including any limitations Mr. Wallace may have but not have yet specified; the job requirements of each of the staff in the section.

— Set out alternative courses of action:
In this case, the space may be divided into one, two or three segments, each of which would be occupied by the appropriate persons. Barbara may like to take advice from the bank's property experts on this.

— Apply a measure of utility to each course of action:
What would be the benefit of each? What would be the drawbacks? For example, separating Margaret off would alleviate any problems arising out of her possible tendency to supervise closely; but it could mean irritating delays as the girls move back and forth for information from her.

— Apply the decision criteria set above:
Given the utility, positive and negative, which solution approaches best the criteria for a good decision? It is at this point that Barbara's logical talent will be engaged, to make an unemotional judgment.

— Select, and project the consequences of a course of action:
Suppose Barbara were to decide on three separate offices: what are the likely consequences in terms of work, and what are the probable reactions of those concerned? Given that these are foreseen, plans can be designed to cope with them.

— Decide, and communicate the decision:
Or possibly more practically in this case, Barbara should recommend the decision she has made, with a clearly set out argument in its favour, to Mr. Wallace, with an action plan for its implementation, with stages and dates. If agreed by him, the plan should be put for information to the staff involved, for their cooperation in implementation.

— Implement and monitor the decision:
Making adjustments to suit the circumstances, although done after the actual decision-making process, is nevertheless closely connected; and Barbara should keep an eye on how the space allocation works out.

**Group Decision Making** The above describes a systematic way of making an individual decision. Barbara could have prefaced her choice of that course of action by a previous decision, of whether to go through the process alone or involve those concerned. A well-read examination candidate could have answered the question using Vroom and Yetton's model, suggesting that Barbara had five possible types of course of action:

AI    Make the decision entirely on her own

AII   Obtain information from the staff and make the decision on her own

CI    Talk to the staff individually and make her own decision

CII   Talk to the staff as a group and make her own decision

GII   Let the staff make their own decision

Which course of action she would choose would depend on:

— The quality of the solution required: is there any solution logically better than another, given company objectives?

— Where does the information lie: with the staff involved?

—    To what extent would they be required to be committed to any solution for its success?

—    Would they accept a decision made by Barbara, whether they actually liked it or not?

—    Do they share the company's objectives or not? And to what extent are they likely to agree with each other?

Depending on the answers to these questions, Barbara would choose between AI, AII, CI, CII and GII, and the question would be answered in similar vein to the suggested courses of action above.

# CASE STUDY 21

For many year your bank has been poorly represented in one of the major towns in an industrial area of England. Although it had two city-centre offices, neither was well-sited and each was housed in cramped, old-fashioned premises. This meant that despite strenuous efforts at developing the branch's business, the bank lagged behind competitors in its standing in the community and in business development.

Some two years ago, after it was decided to merge the two branches, new premises were acquired in the centre of the town's banking sector, and the bank spent a great deal on refurbishing the office to present to existing and prospective customers the image of a modern go-ahead bank.

To complement the change of premises, Mr. Simon Turner was appointed manager of the merged branch. He had a proven record of successful business development, and was aware that his reputation would be greatly enhanced if he made a success of the new venture.

Now, largely due to Turner's drive for new business — and some of his staff have commented on his almost obsessive single-minded approach — the branch has 35% more corporate accounts, and advances have increased to almost double the combined figure of the two old branches, not to mention a massive increase in the number of accounts of personal customers, attracted by the location and the prestigious image of the new premises.

Your boss, the regional manager who is Turner's immediate superior, is delighted by his performance. Recently however he has been less than delighted by an inspection report which has revealed some adverse trends in the standard of clerical work being done at the branch. Backlogs are mounting and piles of work are delayed in a pending stage awaiting completion. There are also some customer complaints about mistakes and delays; and finally the overtime rate, though not yet excessive, is nevertheless climbing relentlessly. The senior inspector has remarked to the manager that the branch is beginning to resemble a vehicle hurtling downhill with a probable case of brake-failure.

Mr Turner, to his credit, is equally concerned, but claims that, in view of his duties to increase business and maintain relationships with existing customers, he and his assistant manager cannot spend excessive amounts of time to sort out clerical problems. He has asked for help from regional office.

The regional manager has asked you and a small team to go to investigate the branch's problems. However, before you go he has asked you to produce a document in which you:

(a) List the possible factors contributing to difficulties at the branch.

(b) Under each factor, list the problems it causes.

(c) For each problem, suggest a tentative set of solutions.

Please draft this document.

# CASE STUDY 21 — MODEL ANSWER

**Problem**

We know that Mr. Turner is a determined, possibly over-enthusiastic business-getter with apparently little interest in routine, who is managing a branch which is the result of a recent merger. The branch has expanded its business at a remarkable rate so that its size and that of its staff must come into consideration. Its routine clerical work is deteriorating, leading to some customer dissatisfaction; and the overtime is rising. The recent inspection report has brought these facts to light.

**Draft Document**

Some factors for consideration would include:

1. **Amalgamation difficulties**

   The branch is still only two years old, formed from two other branches. Though problems have been overcome, in all probability some remain.

   *Possible problems:* Rivalry between cliques formed from the two previous branches; slightly different routines in clerical tasks still not resolved; lack of cohesive team efforts because of lack of leadership; clashes between people who are still relatively new to each other.

   *Solutions:* Section meetings to suggest problem areas and methods of resolving them, possibly held off the premises; careful examination of personnel make-up of sections and teams and review thereof with a view to altering balances. Management involvement in clerical activities and in social activities occasionally to indicate ''oneness' of branch team.

2. **Staffing levels**

   In view of the increased business, staff may be inadequate in numbers, calibre and grade. There may now be too few to service the extra accounts; the complexity of some of the new business may be beyond the capabilities of staff who are unfamiliar with corporate banking; and there may be too few staff with authority to make decisions, thus causing bottle-necks and delays. If new staff have been added, there may have been delays between request and arrival, causing the staff to be forever trying to catch up.

*Possible problems:* Staff trying to cope with excessive amounts of work; complex work waiting for those qualified to handle it, or being handled by inadequately qualified staff; backlogs of work waiting for authorised staff to inspect, or progress, or simply sign.

*Solutions:* Short-term: provide relief staff or team to handle backlog. Medium-term: carefully review staffing levels and needs, including grade-structure, by urgent use of O & M department, making up shortfalls as soon as possible; review staff training and needs. Longer-term: engage in staff training programme to cope with changing and increasing needs of the branch; continuous review of staffing levels and calibre.

3.   **Business development effort**

The manager is devoting all his time and effort to business development, possibly to the detriment of clerical excellence.

*Possible problems:* Ethos which regards business development as exciting and rewarding, clerical accuracy as unimportant leading to unenthusiastic completion of work. Excessive clerical work associated with new accounts. Extra work needed in monitoring new advances taking the attention of officials. Reduction in morale as difficulties are met in giving good service to customers.

*Solutions:* Period of consolidation where additional new business is not intensively sought, and manager devotes attention to servicing existing customers. Business development effort directed towards clerically simple new business. Restructuring of officials' work so that some are in charge of customer service, some of administration and some in charge of business development activities.

**General points**   It would be a pity to dampen Mr. Turner's enthusiasm for new business, but there is no point in gaining some customers, only to lose others because of poor service, or in risking loss to the bank through clerical incompetence.

Any solutions suggested by regional office must be tactful, and should preserve the desire in the staff to contribute increasingly to the bank's development. The problems should be investigated with great care, and the cooperation of all involved, both at the branch and elsewhere in the bank, should be mobilised by regional office.

Finally, Mr. Turner himself needs to be reminded by a senior line manager of the general nature of his own job, and that the technical competence of his branch is ultimately his responsibility and deserves his occasional attention.

# CASE STUDY 22

You have recently been appointed manager of Littletown branch, in succession to Arthur Smith, who has retired after ten years at the branch. In addition to yourself, the staff consists of an assistant manager, Don Brown, who has been there for a year, a chief clerk aged 25, and eight other clerks.

During your first few days, you have established that the staff are enthusiastic, and willing to work hard to achieve the goals you have set for the next few months. They have expressed positive views towards a change in management; and all would be well, except for a problem which has been highlighted by two recent incidents.

In the first, a cheque made payable to a limited company was accepted by a cashier and credited to the personal account of the managing director. No fraudulent act was intended by the latter, and the matter was sorted out; but when you and the assistant manager talked to the cashier she did not understand the significance of the mistake: "It's his company, after all", she said.

In the second incident, the chief clerk had failed to register a charge at Companies House within the statutory period, rendering it worthless as an item of security. The chief clerk, when questioned, admitted openly that he did not know that there was a need to register the charge within a specified time-scale.

Brown, the assistant manager, expressed some initial surprise at these two events. He had considered these and all other members of staff to be reasonably dependable. "To be fair to them, however," he said, "neither has been on a proper training course." He went on to explain that Arthur Smith had been of the strong opinion that formal training courses run at the Regional Training Centre were a waste of time, and that the best way of learning a job was to do it, under the eye of a more experienced colleague. To your horror you have now discovered that, over the last four years, not one single member of staff has been sent on a training course from the branch.

How should you and the assistant manager go about rectifying this situation?

# CASE STUDY 22 — MODEL ANSWER

**Problem**
The inadequate technical knowledge of staff, as a result of exclusively in-branch training can lead to serious problems. There is much to be said for on-the-job training, and people do benefit from being thrown in at the deep end and learning both by doing and by watching others. However, this approach alone has weaknesses:

— Bad or undesirable practices can be passed on if unchecked;

— The experienced operatives to whom the task of training has been given may not be skilled, or enthusiastic about the task of communicating their knowledge,

— The principles underlying the practice may not be conveyed so that the learner may be unable to cope with more complex examples of the work.

— The more unusual aspects of the job may not be covered if they don't happen to occur in the training period.

The consequences of inadequate training can be financial loss, poor reflection on the professionalism of the bank, possible legal infringement, and limits on the career progress of all involved. Action is therefore urgently required in this case.

**Action plan**
1. **Assess the extent of problem**

   Examine job-descriptions, and the actual amount of and extent of training of each member of staff. By using this information, the recent appraisal sheets of the staff, and such knowledge of them as is possessed by the assistant manager, assess the "training gap" between what has been done and what would need to be done to achieve a suitable standard.

   Do not omit to discuss this matter with the individual members of staff, emphasising the intention to improve their technical performance, for their own sake as well as the banks.

2. **Establish training priorities**

   Do this by applying some of these principles, or questions:

   — Inadequacies in whose jobs would cause most damage to the bank/branch?

— Which of the staff suffers from the largest "training gap"?

— Where the training would mean absence from the branch, which of the staff could we manage without for a period? For which could we get relief? How would their absence fit the schedule of holidays and the availability of cover?

3. **Decide whom shall be trained**

An extension of the previous section. Given that more than one person may require the same training, or that some equally valued training may have to be given to one or another, selection may have to be made. Priority may be judged using certain of the following criteria.

— Which is currently doing most of the work?

— Which is brighter/more capable of learning?

— Which would benefit most in the longer-term, with reference to their career prospects and ambitions?

— The training of whom might be more acceptable to the staff themselves, avoiding group tension or rivalries?

— Who, when trained might best pass on the newly gained knowledge or skills to the others?

4. **Establish a branch training programme**

Call in training department and obtain their advice and guidance. Within the above criteria and the constraints of branch procedures and customer service, design a programme involving the integrated use of some of the following:

— Established training courses

— In-branch training under the guidance of a training specialist.

— Special courses developed to meet the needs of certain staff who may not need to attend a complete established course.

— Carefully supervised on-the-job training with advice from training department and the close involvement of the assistant manager.

— The use of video presentations, programmed learning texts, job-guides and the like.

— Secondment for varying periods to appropriate service departments.

5. **Monitor progress**

Before and during the programme the managers must monitor its progress. Staff should be clearly briefed on their own programme and where it fits in. They should join discussions on their progress during and after training. Performance should be systematically examined and judged as the training proceeds. Candidates should be given the opportunity to practice newly-acquired skills, being corrected where there is the danger of mistakes, and positively encouraged where new skills are well-applied.

6. **Future plans**

Formal training programmes should be given a much higher priority than before. The assistant manager should be given the responsibility of organising staff training, to be provided principally from established sources, and to keep up with bank, branch and individual training needs.

# CASE STUDY 23

Western Bank has two offices housing its Trustee Department, approximately 40 miles apart. The question of amalgamating the two offices has often arisen, and it is becoming increasingly evident that significant cost savings can be made from the economies of scale. No firm plans have been made until recently although rumours of merger are rife among staff.

Now, however, the bank branch above which the smaller of the two offices is located, urgently requires extra space to accommodate additional staff and machinery, and the office which Trustee Department occupies would be ideal.

A decision has therefore been taken by the bank executive to close the smaller Trustee branch, which has a staff of 15, and to amalgamate it with the other office, located at bank headquarters and at which 25 Trustee staff work. The executive have discussed this with the two senior managers who are in charge of the branches: they concur with the decision and believe that the efficiency of Trustee Department will be improved by the merger.

It is proposed that the closure of the smaller office and the transfer of the work should take place in eight month's time to coincide with the retirement of the senior of the two managers in charge. Naturally the management and the executive wish to inform the staff fully at a formal meeting at a later stage; but is not surprising that the rumour of the merger spread like wildfire among the staff, and they have demanded an early meeting to discuss the whole matter.

"There are plenty of things we are worried about: the other place is miles away, our manager is retiring, the bank is always trying to cut staff costs — nobody tells us anything, and to be frank, we are angry and frightened", said their unofficial spokesman.

The general manager of Trustee Department agreed to a preliminary meeting to clear the air. Outline the implications of the merger that you think the staff will be most concerned about, and the preliminary response you would recommend to the general manager to each matter concerning them.

# CASE STUDY 23 — MODEL ANSWER

**Problem**   It has become known to staff that the merger is about to take place and a move of some 40 miles is envisaged. Because the meeting to discuss the problems is now arranged before all the answers to all possible problems have been sorted out, the bank can only try to anticipate what would be a reasonable approach to their problems.

The bank will wish to effect the move efficiently, but banks have also traditionally taken the welfare of employees into account as best they can. These two factors and the need to communicate with and to enlist the cooperation of the staff involved will determine the approach to this situation.

Some of the considerations involved in the move which will be of concern to the staff, and the bank's possible response, are:

1. **Redundancy**

   This will be an important matter for the staff, and they will naturally assume that not only offices but jobs might also merge. The general manager will wish to establish as a matter of urgency what the situation is.

   There may indeed be redundancies. He will wish to see to it that the Employment Protection Legislation is complied with, and that the bank's procedures are known to the staff. He may wish to discuss voluntary redundancy.

   There may be none at all planned, and he will wish to convince the staff of this fact, preferably with a written assurance from himself or his superiors.

   It is possible that some might arise after the merger, on a review of the performance of the merged department; and the general manager may want to form a policy for this review and give a realistic forecast of its timing, and its terms: for instance, he may pledge no redundancy but the reduction in jobs by natural wastage.

   If he cannot at this stage make any pledges or policy statements, he will do well to open the debate on these issues frankly, and possibly under the above heads.

### 2.   Move: terms

Each bank has properly negotiated terms for the relocation of staff. Bankwide this is a frequent event, but it will be an experience unfamiliar to most staff.

They will be concerned about what the bank will and will not pay for; what the timing will be; will there be an allowance for "disturbance" and so on. The general manager will want his staff to brief him carefully on this, or to consult the Staff Procedures Manual (candidates answering this question would do well to demonstrate familiarity with their own bank's procedure, not necessarily in detail.

### 3   Move: inability

Some staff, for family or other reasons, may consider themselves simply unable to move. They will want to know the bank's attitude towards this, knowing they have signed a contract of service including a "mobility clause" agreeing to work "where and in what capacity" the bank requires (or words to that effect). However, this is rarely if ever invoked, and people may have aged relatives to care for, or a child at a crucial educational stage, or a spouse unable to transfer employment.

For some of these, relocation into another division of the bank in their home area may be possible. Each of the others will have to be treated individually; and the general manager will wish to inform himself of the bank's likely attitude to them, probably by consultation with senior personnel officers.

### 4.   New staff structure

Concern is likely to be expressed about the new staff set-up in the new office.

Those to be transferred into an existing structure, in particular where the incumbent staff will be supported by their existing senior manager, will fear that their own positions and career development may be prejudiced.

The general manager must provide information on the organisation of staff at the head office; and he may wish to introduce the new manager as soon as possible, well in advance of the merger.

If it is expected that promotions may result as part of the amalgamation, it must be demonstrated that some of the staff of each office gain these promotions.

5.  **Communication & relationships**

The staff of both branches may be in some cases known to each other, but they will all be curious about their new working colleagues. There must be plans made to have them meet each other in advance.

The general manager must be able to pledge, and must press his colleagues, to keep all staff informed of each new development in the move, since ignorance breeds rumours and resentment.

If there are technical matters to be resolved, plans must be seen to have been made to resolve them; and training should be planned to fill any shortfall in staff skills in new or different positions.

Finally, the general manager will realise that morale is important. Given there will be reassurances about the above matters, and that few if any changes in working practices are envisaged, and that the department will be more efficient and effective after the amalgamation, the move can be shown to be positive. If it is dealt with in an enlightened and open manner it could result in the creation of a strong, enthusiastic team in a new larger working group: and the general manager should prepare to convey this effectively.

# CASE STUDY 24

As part of your development, you and two colleagues, Patricia Wilson and Anne Dixon, are to spend a period of intensive training. You are party to a conversation with these trainees which has so far gone as follows: on receiving the news of the secondment, Anne said, "Good — I love course work. I hope we don't have to get involved in all this on-the-job training that is so fashionable these days. You can't learn anything just sitting watching people."

"Nonsense!" exclaimed Patricia; "courses are really boring — sitting there listening to lecture after lecture. However good the speaker is, nobody can concentrate on that sort of thing for hour after hour, day after day. And what have you got at the end of it? A lot of notes about nothing that ever happened in the real world".

"Well, so what?" Anne responded, "The 'real world' isn't so wonderful, and if everyone did everything right out there, there wouldn't be a need for training. If we find ourselves involved in the training department's on-the-job project we'll learn nothing except how it's done, not how it should be done. We'd be much better off on a course."

"I'm sorry, but you're really mistaken", said Patricia. "You don't know what it's like at the training centre. I mean if they had heard of visual aids it might not be so bad; but have you been there recently? They have only just discovered the blackboard!".

"As far as I'm concerned, that's not what's important. A course is what you make it" Anne retorted. "Sitting next to Nellie is no good. They usually don't know you are coming until the day you arrive, they've usually not had to explain their job before, and they are more often than not irritated by you being there looking over their shoulder and blame all the mistakes on you. I had the experience when I first joined, and I don't want it again, thank you".

"Well, I've had enough of courses. Two weeks of airy-fairy theory and no idea of how to cope with real problems, not to mention being bored out of your socks".

At this point they turn to you and ask simultanously "What do you think?"

Set out your considered answer to their query; BRIEFLY outline the advantages and the disadvantages of on-the-job training and course training; and outline what you hope for in the construction of your intensive programme.

# CASE STUDY 24 — MODEL ANSWER

**Problem**  Both colleages seem to have had bad experiences, and are relaying the drawbacks in the two main training methods used in banking. Neither of them are outlining the advantages; and a balanced training programme will combine the best of formal, off-the-job training and work-experience, in a planned and considered manner. A good answer to this question will include a consideration of the advantages and the disadvantages of both types of training, and will suggest a balanced combination for the period of intensive training.

**On-the-job or experimental training**

*Advantages*

| | |
|---|---|
| Relevant | It must be relevant to the work to be done. The links between the training and the work of the office must be demonstrated. |
| Realistic | There must be no problem in rejecting the lessons learnt because they do not relate to the real world |
| Practical | Physical skills are learnt by performing the tasks rather than hearing about them |
| Interesting | To the extent that the job is interesting, people find carrying it out less boring |
| Expertise | If learnt from an expert, the task can be better performed than if learnt from one who knows the elements but has no experience |
| Speed | If part of the learning is on the job, it must be learnt quickly so as to preserve the efficiency of the unit in which it is performed. |

*Disadvantages*

| | |
|---|---|
| Inexpertise | Learning in practice from one who is inexpert, or who practises incorrect methods, develops bad habits |

| | |
|---|---|
| Time | To teach while on the job takes time: unless the involvement of the teacher is whole-hearted, the training task can be resented |
| Instruction | Just because someone does a job well, it does not imply they can teach it adequately |
| Principles | Skill in performing a task is not enough: the principles behind that task should also be learnt |
| Duration | Tasks are often learnt on the job in less time than is planned for the work-experience, and boredom can become a problem. |

**Off-the-job or course training**

*Advantages*

| | |
|---|---|
| Method | What is taught will be "according to the book", will be correct; and should use various media to attract the learning of people with different learning styles. |
| Time | There is no deadline pressure to complete a task on the first occasion: it can be repeated until the skills are learnt. |
| Instruction | Training staff are themselves trained, and have their own objectives in perfecting their training expertise for the benefit of the trainee |
| Principles | There is time for trainers to explain the underlying reasons for actions, so that the trainee will eventually be able to cope with unusual situations |
| Comparisons | With the methods used at the workplace; with the methods used by course-members from other workplaces; sometimes with the methods used by other organisations. |

*Disadvantages*

| | |
|---|---|
| Relevance | It is difficult to make the relevance of seem-ingly minor tasks clear unless the con-sequences of their poor performance is evident. |

| Realism | Simulations are by definition less than real, and this can be made an excuse for poor learning |
|---|---|
| Practicality | Where 'motor' skills are to be learnt, this is not under the pressure of genuine customers or colleagues waiting for the work; the air of lack of urgency can affect motivation |
| Interest | Course work can be boring: lecture periods too long, lack of variety of teaching methods, long periods of concentration on theoretical principles |
| Credibility | For practical people it is often difficult to accord credibility to instructors who are not, sometimes have never been, in the field |
| Time | Courses are generally limited in time, and where practice is necessary, some occasionally do not get their turn. |

**A sensible intensive training programme**
A well-planned programme will have some of these characteristics:

Course work which will instil principles, properly planned and timed at intervals through the programme, with time to reflect and review progress; well taught with a variety of appropriate methods.

On the job training, where the trainers are briefed and warned well in advance, and where they are trained and willing to accept the contributions of trainees; well timed and with specific targets for skill acquisition.

A balance between learning methods with attention given to which method is appropriate to the learning involved.

Above all, clear operational objectives should be set so that progress can be monitored against understood criteria.

It might be added that training is usually more effective when the commitment of the trainee is engaged by the management, whose own commitment should be made clear before, during, and after the training, and by the trainee's attitude of receptiveness to a variety of learning experiences.

# CASE STUDY 25

David Grey is a recently appointed Assistant Lending Officer in Advances Department, responsible for analysing propositions from branch management before referring these for sanction to his Lending Officer. The latter depends heavily on Grey, who is both intelligent and able, with five years' experience of the job.

Over the last few weeks the relationship between the department and Fred Briggs of Stockham branch has deteriorated, since they have declined three applications for new business which Briggs has pursued for some time. On the last occasion, Briggs went for arbitration to the general manager to whom both the branch and the department are responsible. But while the general manager felt that there was merit on both sides, he finally considered the proposition marginal and agreed the department's decision to decline. Briggs had taken this with reasonable grace.

However, a week later Briggs submitted a renewal application for an old established customer who requested the same facility each year though he never used it and operated substantially in credit. Although occasionally accounts have not been produced because of background wealth of knowledge of the track-record, there had never been any hesitation in agreeing the facility. This time, Grey did not follow the usual practice of agreeing the limit and requesting accounts at the earliest convenience, but rather required accounts before the proposition could be recommended to his superior.

This response caused Briggs to lose his temper completely. Since the 'superior' himself, the Lending Officer, was a significant number of grades below Brigg's rank, Briggs felt no compunction in picking up the telephone. He shouted down the Lending Officer's ear:

"I spend all my time trying to get business for this bank, and you people spend all your time losing it because of your Ivory Tower attitude. More often than not your people come straight from college, and after a year at a branch they feel they can, and they do, tell experienced managers how to suck eggs, when they wouldn't know one end of the customer from another. What's more, Grey's attitude is arrogant and unhelpful and you'd better tell him so".

The Lending Officer defended Grey's action in terms of its technical correctness; but he decided to agree the proposition at issue so as to give ground and preserve some form of relationship with Stockham branch.

Discuss the reason why this dispute has arisen, setting it against common problems in line-staff relationships; and suggest ways in which, in the short and longer-term, problems of this nature can be avoided.

# CASE STUDY 25 — MODEL ANSWER

**Problem** — An unconsidered and inconsiderate act on the part of the assistant lending officer.

— An emotional outburst on the part of the branch manager, giving evidence of his views on :

The inexperience in customer contact of the Advances Department.

The relative positions of power, out of line with rank.

Possible views on the place of graduates.

His feelings of frustration in being impeded in his business development activities.

— The decision in favour of the department by the general manager.

**Problem causes** Advances departments are just as interested in the development of new business as are branch staff. However, their function is to take an impersonal, considered view of propositions. They have a depth of technical expertise which the manager does not necessarily possess, and often this expertise is gained without field experience. On the other hand, the branch manager does pick up a width of experience which helps him assess the unquantifiable elements of a proposition better than staff at the centre. This helps him to make mature judgements.

While this tension between the two centres of decision can be useful, it can also occasionally lead to frustration and conflict, as in this case. In addition, it can lead to delay in the process of developing business where speed is sometimes of the essence. There are dangers in this conflict for example:

— The branch manager may seek to set aside the department's instructions, and lend unwisely

— The tension can spread throughout a branch area and wider within the department

— It can affect adversely the customer's relationship with his branch and with the bank as a whole, as he becomes confused as to decision centres

— It will waste time and energy which could be better devoted to pursuing the bank's objectives.

**Suggested actions:**

**Shorter term**

1. The Lending Officer and his assistant should arrange to visit Stockham, and restore reasonable working relationships with Briggs.

2. Arrange a reciprocal visit to the Advances Department for Briggs and possibly his senior staff, to understand by watching the sanctioning process the dangers and possible pitfalls of hasty lending decisions.

3. Ensure that all concerned in the Advances Department are aware of the incident and of the need to preserve relationships with the branches by dealing with requests with tact and consideration.

**Longer term**

1. A programme of reciprocal periods of secondment of line staff to department, and vice versa.

2. A deliberate policy of having department and staff people mix on courses and at conferences so as to reach mutual understanding.

3. Clarify and emphasise responsibility, accountability and authority of both parties, at meetings and in writing, so that there are the minimum of boundary disputes.

4. Career development of senior staff to include substantial periods in both areas to the benefit of both, and the staff member, and the bank as a whole.

# CASE STUDY 26

At Donald Green's branch (which is what he likes to call it, although he is only assistant manager), things have changed. In particular, the clerical standards are now very high, as compared with the sloppy incompetence resulting from his now retired predecessor's slack attitudes. In the six months since Donald has been there, the staff have been very impressed with his technical expertise and standards, and they now look to him for direction whenever they have problems; and on a recent inspection the branch was complimented on its achievement in clerical excellence.

Donald does like having things done his own way, of course. He has achieved his own standards by a "hard slog up through the ranks", and his methods are tried and tested, down to the last trivial detail, on which he insists and which he supervises very carefully. He is not too interested in suggestions from juniors, "wet behind the ears". When they can work free of all errors then he will hear what they have to say, but in the meantime, let them beware of making mistakes in HIS branch, he says firmly.

He is not worried by a certain "him and us" attitude among his staff: he believes that management should be somewhat distanced from the staff: but he is a little puzzled by the incident of the Christmas Party, which came up recently.

In previous years a room had been booked at a local pub, which generally suited everyone. However, Donald Green knew of a better pub, not too far away, where he had been with his previous branch and where the facilities were good and the beer excellent. He mentioned his decision to change the venue, and instructed one of his junior boys to make the booking.

There was an instant mutiny. For no good reason Green could fathom, some of the older women stated point blank that they were not going to the official party, but would have one of their own at the usual pub.

What was worse, one of these women, the manager's secretary, told the manager about it. During this conversation she had told the manager that the atmosphere in the branch was not all it should be, and that Green was causing dissatisfaction and unrest.

On being summoned by the manager and told of all this, Green expressed surprise and regret. He was, after all, acting as he saw fit and he always acted in the best interests of the staff. Everyone should benefit from working in a slick, efficient and effective branch, he said, and the pub he had selected was much better than the usual one. However, he was perfectly happy for them to have the party wherever they liked; and he was quite willing to listen to suggestions as to the way he should relate to the staff.

In view of his willingness to listen to advice, how would you assess Green's management style, and what changes could he make to improve it?

# CASE STUDY 26 — MODEL ANSWER

**Problem**

Green has caused a rebellion against his decision about the venue for the Christmas party; and it has becomed apparent that his relationships with the staff are not happy. This can lead in the future to less effective working as resistance builds up to his personal style and to his methods.

**Causes**

Where the work is centred on an area of the leader's personal expertise, then staff look to him for guidance, and his guidance will be accepted.

However, there are a number of ways of describing Green's style most of which show the negative aspects of operating as he does:

— He is "autocratic". He will not hear suggestions from others and he will have his own methods enforced. Likert would use the term "system 1" for his style.

— He adopts what McGregor would call "Theory X". He believes that the most effective way to motivate his staff is to supervise them closely, because without the fear of punishment they would be unlikely to sustain effort.

— Blake and Mouton would probably find him among the ranks of 9.1, or task-oriented managers, whose concern is for production rather than for people: the job is more important to him both short and long-term than relationships.

— Adair would note that while he pays attention to his group's task need, the group or morale needs are ignored (even countered — the unilateral decision about the pub was calculated to cause dissent) and individual needs seem hardly to be noticed by Green.

— His inflexibility is a problem — lack of what Reddin would refer to as "style-flex": a failure to vary management style according to the situation.

**Suggestions as to changes in style**

These would arise out of assessment, and could be summarised as follows:

— He should understand the need for flexibility. The autocratic style is effective where decisions must be reached quickly: but longer term goals may require consultation or participation for greater effectiveness. The Christmas party issue could have been decided in a context of complete participation by the staff; work method issues are sometimes more effectively resolved if consultation is permitted, and the manager, while making the decisions, nevertheless gives a full hearing to the staff involved. The styles should be adapted to the situation.

— Recognition of the importance of people as well as task, indeed the connection between good relationships and well performed duties. Task-centred leadership has to date paid dividends, but longer-term problems are beginning to appear by way of lower morale and staff opposition. The overlap suggested by Adair between group maintenance and task needs is relevant here: a failure to satisfy the former can lead eventually to a lowering of standards in the latter.

— Managers are not leaders all the time: they must sometimes simply be facilitators for the development of the skills and talents of the individual member of staff. This aspect of the role should be attended to with time and care, and Green would be well advised to look to the needs of each of his team, so as to encourage their personal loyalty and trust.

— The branch manager would be well-advised to take advantage of Green's willingness to learn better managerial methods, should look to planning regular meetings to review his progress, and should monitor and feedback improvements, where they occur and are evident, to Green.

# CASE STUDY 27

The middle of August is the busiest time in the branch of the lively seaside town of Southbourne which receives a large seasonal influx of tourists.

Peter Sand, the manager, has just arrived in the office after a morning visiting customers, to find a lengthy queue of people at the tills. Only three of the five till positions are open, and Sand notices that the three senior cashiers, who normally operate the counter so effectively, are not on duty.

Standing at the back of the banking hall, Sand can tell without difficulty that the three cashiers on duty are very much novices, and while they are operating with courtesy, they look somewhat harrassed at the pressure and concerned at the lengthening queues.

Looking beyond the bandit screen, Sand observes members of staff preparing for an Autumn campaign to increased credit card usage; although there are very few staff at the branch. Some are on holiday, one or two on refresher courses for the September Institute exams, and it is close to lunchtime.

As Sand goes into his office, he calls on Henry Morgan, the assistant manager, to rectify the present situation by diverting two staff from the credit card campaign to the two remaining tills. He then asks Morgan to come in to see him. In the meantime he reflects that Morgan's usual practice is to solve problems by pulling out the stops when a crisis occurs, and that the crisis is often due to Morgan's failure to think ahead.

All this is confirmed when it is discovered during the interview that today's difficulties arise from the coincidence of the annual holiday of two of the senior counter staff while another two have the day off with Morgan's permission.

Peter Sand tells Morgan that unless there is an improvement in organisation and planning, the resonsibility will be removed from Morgan. He asks him to review the shortcomings in his present planning systems and to list ways in which they can be improved.

Outline the points Morgan may cover when preparing the review and the list.

# CASE STUDY 27 — MODEL ANSWER

**Problem**    Morgan fails to plan his staff movements adequately, either in terms of their availability in the office or of their deployment while there. This arises from a lack of sensible planning, and Morgan can review his current situation by asking himself some questions, and then can list paths to improvement.

Review of current situation:

Do I know what I need to plan?

— Staff time and deployment

— Own time and deployment

— Holidays and casual days

— Study leave and examination preparation and execution

— Staff training requirements, including my own

— Business development promotions

— Regular daily work

— Periodic returns

— Other foreseeable events: peak periods, and so on.

Do I use office aids to plan?

— Branch card diary system to remind of events/duties

— Personal diary and list of tasks day-to-day

— Year-planner or other wider-view system for holidays, etc.

— Rota's posted on notice boards.


Do I set time aside to plan carefully?

— Take steps to plan and diary stages for monitoring

— Face up to oncoming crises and think in advance of solutions

— Delegate some planning/monitoring tasks to subordinates

— Communicate plans to others in the office

— Ensure that tasks are done by those most competent

— Ensure that planned training guarantees succession and cover.

116

**Methods of improvement**

Improvement will depend on determination to alter behaviour wherever any of the above questions are answered by "no". Morgan should:

— Determine to make planning a high priority task
— Set time aside daily for the exclusive purpose of planning
— Establish effective physical systems for monitoring, e.g. an effective diary/year-planner system for holidays
— Review the skills and talents of his staff and plan training.

Enlist the help of others:

— Mr Sand, to help and advise on the new plans
— The staff, to cooperate for the sake of the branch in any altered work practices
— Training department, to help him plan the development of his staff and of his own managerial skills.

Mr. Sand should listen carefully to Morgan's review, and discuss his proposals, adding, revising or altering where expedient. He should establish deadlines and monitor progress towards new systems. He should by his attitude and behaviour positively encourage Sand to become a more effective manager along the lines he is proposing.

# CASE STUDY 28

You are the manager of a branch with a staff of 17 persons, including three cashiers and an enquiry clerk. Directly responsible to you are:

a.  Arthur, the branch accountant — a man of 48 who has occupied this position for many years before you were appointed.

b.  Bernard, an Assistant Manager Lending.

c.  Charles, an Assistant Manager in charge of administration. This manager is a young man, a graduate, who has reached this position after accelerated training. A natural innovator, very keen on new technology, who expects everybody to share his enthusiasm for adopting new methods.

Mechanisation of the branch has mainly taken place during the preceding two years, since Charles' appointment. Charles professes himself to be keen on his staff participating in decision making, but resents any suggestions which appear to impede the immediate use of new equipment. The staff are continually complaining about the noise, which is caused by typewriters, telephones, cheque sorting and printing, and other machines. These are all placed conveniently near the staff using them, in one fair sized room. Another, slightly smaller room contains the records and stores.

Serious errors are occurring because parts of telephone conversations with head office and customers are drowned by background noise. Time is being wasted by having to repeat work and placate the customers. Similar errors occur internally because parts of conversations are drowned. Irritation has also grown steadily between the people concerned, and relations among the staff are steadily deteriorating.

Comparison with figures for the earlier years shows that absenteeism due to minor illness has increased significantly. So has the number of members of staff applying for transfers. When staff requesting transfers are asked for their reasons, worsening working conditions at the branch are invariably cited.

At a meeting called to identify the reasons for the increase in customers' complaints, Arthur firmly blames the new machines. Bernard feels that lower staff morale is to blame, while Charles says that the staff are simply stick-in-the-muds, who will soon get used to the new equipment. After that the complaints will cease.

What action can be taken to improve the situation?

# CASE STUDY 28 — MODEL ANSWER

**Problem**     The apparent problems can be summarised as follows:

(a)   excessive noise

(b)   reduced output

(c)   loss of customer goodwill

(d)   increased absenteeism

(e)   falling staff morale.

The requests for transfers are a clear indiciation that one of Herzberg's Hygiene Factors is not being met — in this case it would be "working conditions", or "unsatisfactory supervision". The latter is exemplified by the difference in attitude which the supervisors have towards new technology.

Perhaps the first step should be to review the procedure for introducing new technology, to check that adequate warning, explanation, and training are given.

It appears that the increased noise from machinery could well be the real problem. To be on the safe side it would however be advisable to seek further information on other possible causes, e.g. whether there is concern over possible redundancies, or whether local wage rates have run ahead of those of the bank.

Enquiries should also be made about the incidence of similar problems in other branches, and how effective various solutions have proved.

Information should be sought on the correct noise levels of the machinery to eliminate the possibility of maintenance or other special factors being at the root of the problem.

The key issues are:

—   to obtain the full benefits from the mechanisation

—   to eliminate the risk of further falls in output due to falling morale

—   to restore morale to previous levels

—   how to avoid a recurrence of such a situation.

**Solution**       Possible solutions for improving the present situation:

Establish a problem-solving group consisting of the three assistant managers (to provide different points of view), one or two clerks to represent the staff, and the manager to control meetings and integrate all views. This group would consider such options as:

(a)    Taking out the noise-producing machines.

It would be a dangerous and quite unwarranted assumption that mechanisation can never be reversed, but in this case the branch would almost certainly have to fit in with the systems of the bank as a whole. A possible drop in productivity would also have to be considered.

This solution could, therefore, only take the form of a proposal to head office.

(b)    Reducing the noise level of the equipment.

It is sometimes possible to adapt machines, the bases on which they stand, or the acoustic of the environmental space, to reduce noise. The feasibility and cost of this solution should be investigated.

(c)    Reorganisation of the work lay-out.

If all machines are moved into the second room and switched with the records, etc. the main noise would be eliminated.

The telephones could either be muted, or better still a small branch exchange could be installed, thus eliminating the ringing noise of incoming calls completely. This solution would also make it possible for some records to be sited more conveniently for the staff using them.

*Disadvantages* — cheques and other documents might have to be moved frequently and longer distances.

A clerk would probably have to be up-graded to take charge of the machine-room.

(d)   Solution (c) is favoured because it is most likely to be successful with the minimum of cost.

(e)   Before attempting to implement this solution advice should be sought from O & M department. It must be carefully planned to avoid interrupting normal work.

(f)   After a period the indicators of effectiveness considered above should be reviewed to confirm that the desired improvements have been achieved.

(g)   Solutions to avoid similar problems in future:

Create awareness of technological developments through news-sheets, presentations, etc. before such developments reach the branch.

Encourage contacts with other branches already using new equipment.

Maintain the "problem solving group" to plan innovation more carefully.

# CASE STUDY 29

The foreign department of a large city centre branch has as its clients the 20 smaller branches in the town, and about 60 corporate customers. The services they provide include travel facilities, foreign currency transfers and accounts.

Dennis, the assistant manager in charge, organises the department so that three clerks are responsible for dealing with customers. Four clerks process the instructions, and two typists provide general assistance.

Dennis's relationship with the permanent members of his staff is good, but he resents clerks being periodically withdrawn and replaced by others for training. Particularly if they are on accelerated training courses, he cannot be bothered to deal with their problems and would rather deal with queries relating to their work himself.

Complaints are regularly received from customers about delays and failure to carry out instructions correctly, or at all. Considerable time is wasted in trying to correct and trace the cause of these mistakes, for which no one is ever willing to take the blame. It has, however, been confirmed that mistakes often occur for the following reasons:

— Customer instructions misunderstood by enquiry clerk.

— Messages not passed on from enquiry clerk.

— Message not clear.

— Errors in messages.

— Instructions misunderstood by processing clerks.

— Uncertainty about which clerk took the instruction.

— Confusion about which processing clerk is handling a particular job.

— Customers' changes not directed to the right clerk.

— Mistakes made by typist transcribing material received from processing clerks.

Consider this problem and make recommendations for reducing the number of mistakes.

# CASE STUDY 29 — MODEL ANSWER

**Problem**

1. The symptoms of the problem seem to be:

   Delays and mistakes in executing customers instructions.

2. What problems might have caused such symptoms?
   — Uninterested staff
   — Lack of training
   — Work overload
   — Organisation of work
   — Lack of staff ability.

3. The workload of the department should be compared to similar departments to establish the validity of this cause.

   Such a comparison would also give information on the motivation of the staff. Information should also be sought on the training received by new staff before they join the department, and their abilities should be assessed to ensure that they are up to the standard required for the work.

4. The attitude of Dennis to new staff is a problem to be dealt with first, as it could well be the cause of many of the symptoms. The importance of training as part of his role should be explained and made part of his objective. If this is ignored he should if necessary be penalised.

5. If the above factors are eliminated, the other problem in this situation becomes the correct receipt and transfer of information from person to person. This requires:

   a. Improved understanding of customers' instructions.

   b. Improved communication between enquiry, processing and typing staff.

**Solution**     1.   Re-organise the work flow so that customers whose names begin with letters A-F will all be dealt with by a regular team of one enquiry clerk, one processor and one typist. Two other teams would be assigned to other specified customers. This would enable each team to learn to know their customers' needs and therefore improve understanding. Communication would be improved because the source and destination of messages is known, there would be more incentive for team members to help each other as mistakes are directly attributable to the team responsible for that customer.

If newcomers are properly integrated into the teams their training and performance will be improved. The fourth processing clerk will be available to cover peak loads for any team. He could also be used to integrate the newcomers.

A disadvantage of this solution is a certain inflexibility, especially as customers might sometimes have to wait for their contact clerk.

2.   All messages to be signed and retained. This would only solve some of the problems and involve a lot of extra work.

3.   Each clerk could combine taking enquiries and processing for a smaller number of clients. This does mean retraining all of them in a wider range of skills.

Solution (1) is favoured as it offers the greatest likelihood of success with the least additional cost. If adopted, the number of complaints in comparison with the earlier method must be checked regularly.

Senior management has to expect some deterioration in performance if it "interferes" with the running of departments, switching staff or imposing extra duties such as training.

# CASE STUDY 30

Bernard Bainbridge is forty-two years old. He has worked for the bank since the age of sixteen when he left school with very good 'O' levels. He married at the age of twenty-four and moved into a house in the suburb of the city where he has always lived and worked. He now has three children. He has never moved house and, although he has worked in one or two sub-branches, for most of his working life he has held a variety of jobs in the main city branch. His career has been marked by solid achievement rather than spectacular success. He was regarded as an excellent clerk. He was very reliable and responsible. He made few errors and always hit deadlines. His colleagues regarded him as a very solid and dependable worker who could be relied on to manage routine work very well. Ultimately he was promoted to lead a processing section. He was very familiar with the work and had no problems in organising it, training his staff, getting them to work hard and to produce results. Non-routine decision sometimes caused him problems, but he had a sympathetic boss who was always ready to take difficult decisions.

A year ago the bank went through a considerable reorganisation. The result was that much more authority was delegated from the centre to improve the service to customers. Changes took place in the branch to reflect the new policy and as a result Bernard was promoted to a new job. This included the supervision of a processing section but also included work which involved making decisions in relation to loans where considerable initiative was left to the supervisor, with the support of a very capable and experienced staff.

After a few months the manager noticed some ominous signs. Bernard began to look pale and drawn. He worked overtime systematically, although previously it was possible to set one's watch by his arrival and departure times. He was the most equable of men, but now he began to show signs of irritation and bad temper. He also took work home and came back with it uncompleted the next day. His department still functions well, especially the area concerned with processing. But those subordinates who work on loans complain that Bernard constantly intervenes in their decisions, or dithers about those which are referred to him. This sometimes wastes so much time that the business goes to another bank. Already one staff member has requested a transfer. He says that he is bored by making routine decisions and is not allowed to get involved in the more interesting ones. He has lost interest in the work. Others also feel frustrated and this feeling is communicating itself to the processing group where there has been a small but noticeable increase in absenteeism and a marginal decline in productivity.

What is happening? If you were Bernard's manager what would you do?

MR BAINBRIDGE'S INDECISION IS FINAL

# CASE STUDY 30 — MODEL ANSWER

**Problem**     Slow decision making causing backlogs and, in at least one case, a loss of business. A decline in morale as a result of over-supervision, boring work, shown by increasing labour turn-over and higher absenteeism.

**Cause**     The root of the problem lies in a change of policy involving the delegation of decisions coupled with the simultaneous promotion of Bernard to a new job where he is worried by the decision-making, he does not delegate work and oversupervises his staff.

**Analysis**     The evidence:

Bernard's success with routine, his reliability, his unchanging life style, his concern with order, all suggest high security needs. People with these needs usually cope well in conditions of relative stability where rules are clear, the level of work is predictable and decisions are routine.

Now Bernard finds himself having to make non-routine decisions frequently and this clearly causes him trouble — viz. the overtime, taking work home, irritability, etc.

Unless he can learn to delegate work he will make himself ill and reduce the effectiveness of the section.

**Action**     The manager must therefore try to help Bernard to delegate work to his staff which is clearly within their capacity. To do this the manager must persuade Bernard that:

—     his subordinates are perfectly capable of taking decisions and do not need to be so closely supervised.

—     they can be trained to take many of the decisions now taken by Bernard.

—     that he will then be freed to plan and organise the flow of work more effectively and he will reduce pressure on himself.

To achieve this the manager should get Bernard

(i)     to identify staff who are capable of development